Wyndham Lewis

Wyndham Lewis

by Jane Farrington

with contributions by Sir John Rothenstein

Richard Cork

Omar S. Pound

Lund Humphries · London   *in association with the City of Manchester Art Galleries*

Copyright © 1980 City of Manchester Cultural Services

First edition 1980
Published by
Lund Humphries Publishers Ltd
26 Litchfield Street London WC2

SBN 85331 434 9

Designed by Herbert Spencer
Filmset by Keyspools Ltd. Golborne, Lancs
Printed and bound by Lund Humphries, Bradford, Yorks

Front cover: *Portrait of the Artist as the Painter Raphael*, 1921 (cat.78)
Back cover: *Mamie*, 1911 (cat. 6)
Frontispiece: Wyndham Lewis in his studio
photographed by Alvin Langdon Coburn in February 1916

This is the catalogue of the exhibition 'Wyndham Lewis'
held at the Manchester City Art Gallery
from 1 October to 15 November 1980
and subsequently at the National Museum of Wales, Cardiff
from 29 November 1980 to 11 January 1981
and at the City Art Centre, Edinburgh
from 23 January to 7 March 1981.
This exhibition was organised by Manchester City Art Gallery
with financial assistance from the Arts Council of Great Britain.

Contents

Foreword

by Timothy Clifford

This is the first major exhibition devoted to Wyndham Lewis since the retrospective at the Tate Gallery in 1956. It has been made possible by the generosity of owners, both public and private, who, in many cases, have also allowed their works to be included in the exhibition's tour to the National Museum of Wales, Cardiff, and the Art Centre, Edinburgh. Some owners have lent from their collections extensively and in this respect I should like to thank especially the Tate Gallery, the Victoria and Albert Museum, the Vint Trust and Omar S. Pound.

We are most grateful to Sir John Rothenstein for writing the introduction and also to Richard Cork and Omar S. Pound for their important contributions. Many people have given practical help and enthusiastic support. We should especially like to thank J.W.Dolman, C.J.Fox and O.S.Pound, trustees of the estate of the late Mrs Gladys Anne Wyndham Lewis, Andrew Murray of the Mayor Gallery and Chris Mullen, who have both made generous loans from their private collections of Wyndham Lewis first editions, Elizabeth Ayrton, the Hon. David Bathurst, D.G.Bridson, David Brown, J.F.Cullis, David Drey, David Hughes, Richard Humphries, Nicholas Mann, Professor Jeffrey Meyers, Walter Michel, Naomi Mitchison, Stella Newton, Anthony d'Offay, Helen Peppin, Sir Sacheverell Sitwell Denys Sutton, Julian Symons, Dame Rebecca West and Josephine Whitehorn. We should also like to thank David Fraser Jenkins and Elizabeth Cumming for co-operating with us so fully over the exhibition tour.

The greatest debt of gratitude goes to Jane Farrington, Assistant Keeper in the Fine Arts Department, who has selected the exhibits, written the catalogue and supervised all the arrangements. Her great enthusiasm for Wyndham Lewis has been most contagious.

Introduction

by John Rothenstein

When I was honoured by the invitation to write the introduction to the catalogue of this exhibition I recklessly accepted. Wyndham Lewis was an artist I had long ardently admired; also a friend. I agree with the opinion that T.S.Eliot once expressed, that he was the most fascinating personality of our time.[1]

The organisers of the exhibition have been wise to include besides paintings and drawings, his books, pamphlets and magazines. For all have a degree of unity. To take a passage almost arbitrarily from his writings about art: 'To begin with, I hold that there never was an *end*; everything of which our life is composed, pictures and books as well as anything else, is a means only, in the sense that the work of art exists in the body of the movement of life. It may be a strong factor of progress and direction, but we cannot say that it is . . . the end or the reason of things, for it is so much implicated with them; and when we are speaking of art we suddenly find we are talking of life all the time.'[2]

This comprehensive concept took time to evolve. When he was a student at the Slade, where he won a scholarship (from 1899 until 1901) according to my father, who befriended him, 'He hesitated between writing and painting'.[3]

I mention this relationship principally because it characterises a singular feature of Lewis's early life, namely how little known, indeed how virtually unknown, this boy and youth of high intelligence and original character was in his early years. According to Geoffrey Wagner, 'The only published Slade School memoir . . . of Lewis we have is from Sir William Rothenstein,'[4] although his talents both as poet – he was nicknamed 'Lewis the Poet' – and draughtsman attracted some recognition, both from fellow-students and established writers such as Laurence Binyon and Sturge Moore.

And as for Rugby no member of the School appears to have heard of him, which is not altogether surprising as he was placed twenty-sixth in a class of twenty-six and left aged sixteen.

Soon after leaving the Slade he spent some eight years on the Continent, in Munich, Madrid – sharing a studio with Spencer Gore – Brittany and elsewhere, and much time in Paris. In Munich, a notable centre of the visual arts, he spent six months at the Heimann Academy, and considerably longer in Paris, having a studio in the Rue Delambre, where besides leading a lively bohemian life he read widely, attended Bergson's lectures at the Collège de France and became acquainted with a number of artists and intellectual figures, assimilating the ideas of anti-romantic thinkers, Laserre, Massis, Seillière and Sorel among them.

When he returned to England in 1909 he was, therefore, unusually conversant with the artistic and intellectual life of the Continent, which he used to full advantage in both his art and writings. He returned, in fact, a formidable figure. Many of his works were tentative, but those such as *The Starry Sky* (cat.20) of 1912, and *Planners* (cat.33) of 1913, the one Cubist and the other Abstract, quickly established his reputation. Although eventually he became critical of Abstraction, his own work before the First World War mostly partook, in varying highly personal forms, of its character. To cite two among numerous examples, *Composition* (cat.26) and *Portrait of an Englishwoman*, both of 1913, the second at the Wadsworth Atheneum, Hartford, Connecticut, USA.

Lewis's version of the prevailing Abstraction was Vorticism, which he thus defined '"Vorticism" accepted the machine-world: that is the point to stress. It sought out machine-forms. The pictures of the Vorticists were a sort of *machines* . . . It was cheerfully and dogmatically external . . . [It] was not an asylum from the brutality of mechanical life. On the contrary it identified itself with that brutality, in a stoical embrace, though of course without propagandist fuss.

It did not sentimentalize machines . . . it took them as a matter of course: just as we take hills, rivers, coal deposits . . . as a matter of course. It was a stoic creed: it was not an *uplift* . . .'[5]

His contributions to the two editions of *Blast*, published in 1914 and 1915 (fascinating as his magazines appear today, none of them, either *Blast*, or the later *Tyro* or *The Enemy* survived more than two or three issues) represented the culmination of his militant and highly personal pre-war convictions, but in the period between his return to England and the First World War his activities as a militant pioneer, painter and draughtsman were intense, and – especially his formidable Cubist geometrics – won him greater fame than he enjoyed during any other period, except during the last years, of his life. 'Our most articulate voice' was how Pound described him.

The years immediately preceding the war were cosmopolitan and revolutionary, but complex though their history was, it is not unreasonable to describe Vorticism – the term was invented by Ezra Pound – as its culmination in Britain. The impact of Vorticism and its sensational publications – both in looks and contents – *Blast*, the 'Review of the Great English Vortex' was immense, although on the relatively small 'revolutionary' section of the London art world. Lewis, its creator, could afford language that seemed violent and extreme, though reading it today it is clear that it is also marked by much wisdom – also wit. Visitors to the exhibition will be able to see *Blast*, so I will not quote from it except a sentence from No.2 which seems as well as any other to define its purpose:

> 'Blast and Vorticism
> In Vorticism, the direct and hot
> impressions of *life* are mated with
> abstraction, or the combination of the *Will*'

The war interrupted the vigorous movements and activities – there were of course a number besides Vorticism – that reached their climax in the year of its outbreak. It had, however, a radical effect on the art of Lewis. Shortly after its outbreak he was ill, but during intervals of recovery he began *Tarr* – his first and one of his most impressive novels – helped to prepare the first number of *Blast* published in late June, and made several paintings as well as organising the first and only Vorticist Exhibition held in June 1915; *Blast No. 2* was published in July. The intervals of recovery must have been frequent or prolonged!

In March 1916 Lewis joined the Royal Artillery and was commissioned at the end of the year, his battery moving to the Front line near Bailleul in July the following year, and in December he was commissioned as an Official Artist to the Canadian War Memorials at their Corps Headquarters at Vimy Ridge.

This appointment highly stimulated this immensely industrious artist, and, although painfully conscious of its calamitous character, he was enraptured by the splendour of mechanical warfare. Big guns in particular possessed the characteristics of power, hardness, purposefulness and unqualified masculinity, that marked his own temperament. In the presence of big guns the place of satire was usurped by romance.

He wrote: '. . . if out of the campaign in Flanders any material, like the spears in Uccello's *Battle* in the National Gallery, force themselves on the artist's imagination, he will use it. The huge German siege guns, for instance, are a stimulus to the vision of power'. 'Great guns are just as magnificent as are unwieldy spears of armoured cavaliers. The guns were at all events my choice. I was not associating myself with a more imposing object than a six-inch howitzer; but I made what I could out of that.'[6]

'Gaudier-Brzeska was killed in action within 6 months of the outbreak of war – that was a very great loss to the art of sculpture; Hulme, the philosopher – journalist of "abstraction" in 1914 was killed in action in 1917, only a few hundred yards from my own gun – his battery was in sight of ours, a few hundred yards to the right, in the soggy coast plain behind Nieuport in Flanders. The sergeant of my gun was killed and most of my guncrew made casualties, during the same prolonged bombardment, which was the German answer to our preparations to attack.'[7]

Lewis's war experiences have been emphasised on account of their radical effect on his art. Cubism, from which Vorticism was predominantly derived, proved a mode of expression inadequate to represent the emotions that these experiences aroused.

'The Geometrics which had interested me so exclusively before', he wrote, 'I now felt were bleak and empty. *They wanted filling*. They were still as much present in my mind as ever, but submerged in the coloured vegetation, the flesh and blood, that is life . . .'[8] He also wrote 'War, and especially those miles of hideous desert known as "the Line" in Flanders and France, presented me with a subject-matter so consonant with the austerity of that "abstract" vision I had developed, that it was an easy transition.'[9]

Lewis's suggestion that in his war paintings and drawings, he was filling his geometrics, gives a very inadequate notion of the extraordinary power of representing natural forms which manifests itself in the work he did from about 1918.

Yet there is one significant respect, an element of fact, in his assertions that 'The geometrics . . . were still as much present in my mind' and 'the austerity of that "abstract" vision I had developed'. In so far as it is possible to make so radical a generalisation about the work of an artist whose oeuvre is varied and extensive – there survive about a hundred paintings and a thousand drawings – the more linear, more angular they are the finer. Of his war work the most impressive is *A Battery Shelled* (see p. 73), an oil of 1919 at the Imperial War Museum. Here the geometrics *are* filled to make an impressive, legible work, yet geometrics they remain. The muddy ground, several of the figures, and even, astonishingly, the smoke of the explosions, are 'geometrics', yet they hardly affect the 'realism' of the work, so effectively are they 'filled'.

Lewis made a considerable number of drawings and a few paintings in the 1930s, particularly portrait heads, of a relatively conventional character, for instance, *Naomi Mitchison* (cat.137) of 1938, but he is at his most characteristic and impressive in those which have a greater or a lesser degree of his Cubist structure, such as *Combat No. 3* (cat.36) of 1914; *Mr Wyndham Lewis as a Tyro* (cat.80) and *A Reading of Ovid* (cat.81), both of 1920–1; *Ezra Pound* (cat.61) of 1919, *The Surrender of Barcelona* (cat.130) of 1936, *Inferno*, oil of 1937, at the National Gallery of Victoria, Melbourne; *Edith Sitwell* (cat.113) of 1923–35, and *A Portrait of Ezra Pound* (cat.143) of 1939; *Red Portrait* (cat.134) of 1937 and *Head of Ezra Pound* (cat.145) of 1939.

There is an extremely curious contrast between Lewis's portraits in oil and pen and his treatment of his subjects in his writings. His *Men without Art* is virtually a deadly bombardment of a number of his subjects, Hemingway, Faulkner, Eliot, Henry James, Virginia Woolf among them, and in *The Apes of God* it is so ferocious that he dared not name them, recognisable though they are.

Take by way of example a single subject: his paintings of Eliot, those at Harvard, at the Municipal Art Gallery, Durban, South Africa (cat.147), both of 1938, and at

Magdalene College, Cambridge, of 1949. All three are benevolent likenesses, whereas Eliot had surely never before been the subject of so ferocious an attack as in *Men Without Art*. Why this disparity, almost absolute, between the painted and written image?

I believe Lewis was a triple personality. As a writer the most formidable, the fiercest critic of our time. He used to assert, often in conversation and occasionally in print, that he was compelled to write in order to justify his art. But this was not so. Whether his painting and drawing or his writing is his major achievement is for posterity to judge, but they are at least comparable. (Eliot called him 'The most distinguished English novelist'.[10]) Apart from his brief reviews of exhibitions written during the 1940s and 1950s for *The Listener* in which the frequent use of 'heavy guns' would have been unacceptable – and in any case he was apt to be benevolently disposed to the gifted among his juniors – his use, of 'heavy guns' elsewhere was frequently devastating.

His portraits, paintings and drawings, on the contrary – apart from a number of Vorticist or near-Vorticist figures of the 1920s, such as *Mr Wyndham Lewis as a Tyro*, already mentioned – are scarcely ever caricatures and are mostly, in any case, of anonymous subjects. Almost all his portraits – at least of the subjects known to me, and many are, personally or from photographs – are sympathetic though precise likenesses. Lewis was the devastating critic in his writings and the usually sympathetic but sometimes detached portrayer of his fellow men and women.

What of the man? As he has been dead for almost a quarter of a century there cannot be many still around who knew him.

I well remember our first meeting. It was in the early 1920s and my parents were entertaining some friends at their house in Kensington. Taking the only vacant chair I found myself sitting next to a man whose dark eyes, thick black hair, black scarf and long overcoat heightened the pallor of his face. Hearing that I was an undergraduate at Oxford he questioned me about the intellectual life there, and when I spoke of the intelligence of some of my friends he said, 'I suppose they must be a lot of fools'. I asked coldly who he was. 'Wyndham Lewis', he answered. 'Then you're the author of *Tarr*!' I exclaimed, 'one of the best contemporary novels I've read.' This seemed to please him, we became friends and met at intervals until the end of his life.

His conversation ranged very widely. Unlike his writing, in which he was prone to show the incomparably deadly claws of his satire, his talk was sometimes expressive of suspicion that this person or that was plotting to do him an injury, but in general it was perceptively benevolent. The defensive element in his character, however, expressed itself not only in his talk but in his way of life: his dwellings, too, were defensive. At Adam and Eve Mews, off Kensington High Street, where he lived when I first came to know him, his room was difficult to find, likewise that in Percy Street, while at studio A, 29 Kensington Gardens Studios, where he mostly lived in his later years, his rooms, along a bare passage at the top of a stone staircase, were almost impossible to find – even after a previous visit. Just before the War I dined there with him: the meal was elaborate and the studio impeccable and I was reminded of eating – it could not be called dining – at Percy Street sometime before when we had sat on packing-cases in front of a red-hot iron stove from whose angry rays we would have suffered had we not been shielded by a yard-high range of cinders. I was naturally puzzled.

We met from time to time and I am in his debt for his learned clarification of various aspects of art and literature.

On 1 October 1939, with my wife and daughter I left for an official visit to the USA – to arrange for the exhibition and subsequent safekeeping of the British pictures at the New York World's Fair and other assignments there and in Canada.

A few moments after I had arrived on a visit to Buffalo I was handed a note asking me to call at the Stuyvesant Hotel. 'I think you know my wife', he said genially, introducing me to a woman whom I recognised as the handsome 'Froanna' of several of his portraits, knowing well that not only had we never met but that he had never mentioned her.

My wife invited Lewis to spend Christmas with her parents and us in Lexington, Kentucky. As I had neglected to make the situation clear, he wrote to her, from the Tuscany Hotel, New York on 21 December 1939: 'We (I have a wife and dog with me) are going just outside N.Y. to Connecticut for the New Year beano. (You say you never know whether people are married or not. My wife and I were most orthodoxly spliced a long time ago. But life has been somewhat of a war for me, and the warrior – the Gauls being an exception – has usually kept the field of battle free of females. Man's domestic nature is stressed here in your American matriarchy and I have found myself rather overshadowed by my wife, as a fact, and she has been forced a little into the fray. – We have no children. She is blonde, she tends to put on fat, her mother was German, her father a good British farmer and as straight as a gun-barrel; she has ridden all over the Atlas on a mule and is a great reader of my books: but you can see she is a wife in a thousand).'[11]

After my return to London we corresponded but after his own return in 1946, due to exceptional demands on my time owing to the restoration of the bomb-damaged Tate and an exhibition of its works which toured Europe, and much besides, I saw him rarely. But in May 1951, distressed by a tragic article in *The Listener* 'The Sea-Mists of Winter', in which he announced his blindness, I wrote to him and received this touching reply: 'I have been over to Ireland which is why I have been so long in answering your letter. I have received many letters about my approaching blindness but hardly any which I found affected me so much, in its simple sincerity – your words about Rude Assignment gave me great pleasure: You are au courant in the matter of its subject, which makes your opinion doubly valuable.'[12]

His near-blindness and the poor state of his health which aggravated his morbid obsession with the supposed hostility of his fellow men (the more influential – the more hostile) determined me to propose to our Trustees, what I had long had in mind, that we should arrange a retrospective exhibition of his work at the Tate – none had ever been held. They readily agreed and he wrote a brief foreword to the catalogue. At the private view was a remarkable assembly of old friends – and enemies. Eliot, the Sitwells, Kate Lechmere (who had paid for *Blast* and the Rebel Art Centre) were among those present. It was I fancy the last occasion when the survivors of the movement in which he had played so splendid a part were gathered together.

Lewis was so exhausted by the ordeal that it was only with difficulty that his wife, mine and I, could get him into a taxi – exhausted, but touchingly happy. There were tears in his eyes.

[1] *The Egoist*, September 1918
[2] *The Tyro No. 2*, 1924, p.22
[3] William Rothenstein, *Men and Memories*, vol.2, 1933, p.27
[4] Geoffrey Wagner, *Wyndham Lewis*, 1957, p.6
[5] W. Lewis, *Wyndham Lewis the Artist: from 'Blast' to Burlington House*, 1939, p.78
[6] Ibid., p.69
[7] Ibid., pp.68–9
[8] Lewis, *Rude Assignment*, 1950, p.129
[9] Ibid., p.128
[10] *The Hudson Review*, Winter 1955
[11] Sir John Rothenstein, *Brave Day, Hideous Night*, 1966, p.68
[12] Letter dated 9 July 1951, reprinted in Sir John Rothenstein, *Time's Thievish Progress*, 1970, pp.37–8

Wyndham Lewis: an assessment

by Jane Farrington

Wyndham Lewis was too good at too many things to fit happily into a history of twentieth-century British art. In an age of specialisation, his public found it hard to understand an artist whose creative output was devoted equally to painting and to writing. In his first autobiography, he considered it necessary to justify his multiple talents, when he wrote: 'I am a novelist, painter, sculptor, philosopher, draughtsman, critic, politician, journalist, essayist, pamphleteer, all rolled into one, like one of those portmanteau-men of the Italian Renaissance.'[1] Writing played an equal and, certainly in the later years, a dominant rôle in Lewis's career, but he regarded himself first as an artist. In a letter to Leonard Amster he stated: 'My trade is painting. Many of my books are merely a protest against Anglo-Saxon civilisation, which puts so many obstacles in the way of the artist.'[2] Lewis's increasing bitterness and frustration at the hostility, or – worse – indifference, of his public formed his belief that 'The English will never regard painting as anything but a joke, or a chocolate box.'[3]

At his best, Lewis produced masterpieces of extraordinary power, but his continually straitened means and long periods of illness forced him to produce pot-boilers, both in painting and writing. Well over a thousand drawings survive but far too many are dreary rows of society portraits, produced to keep the wolf from the door. Far fewer paintings remain: a little over one hundred. In the case of portraiture, there is a considerable difference in time and effort between a drawing and a painting. Lewis wrote: 'If it is your purpose to do a *good* portrait – I mean one not too indecently pretty, or merely photographic, you will almost invariably have a free fight with your sitter (or her husband or his wife) at the end of it. Unless you are a jolly good businessman you will have the portrait on your hands. Under these circumstances it is obviously better not to undertake an oil-portrait which is going to eat up a good deal of your time. If it is a pencil head, which has only occupied two or three afternoons, that doesn't matter so much.'[4]

Lewis's early oils are often on a large scale, but this is not true of any of the later paintings. In a letter of 1933 to Sydney Schiff, he wrote: 'during the years that I have been writing books I have still produced spasmodically (and as my books achieved notoriety, have sold) pictures and drawings, usually small, (as in a small room it is difficult to paint a large picture) . . . The new work I have been completing (and which you expressed yourself as interested to see) I have had to do on a chair, for the simple reason that I have not, since my illness, had the money to spare to buy the necessary easel.'[5]

Lewis, a great painter, was one of the most important figures in British art of the first half of this century. However, he never realised his full potential as an artist or writer, and he knew it. In 1940, he wrote: 'I regard anything as *waste* that is not spent in giving the fullest play possible to a person's aptitudes, and mine are very marked in all the arts except music. At present I am a *painter without a workshop*, and a writer who is capable of such productions as the *Childermass* forced to write – well, very jolly stuff, but not providing such a scope as nature clearly intended. – However, we all waste our lives. I reckon I waste 99 per cent of mine, without ever getting reconciled to it.'[6]

Lewis was a late starter. In 1914, the year that Vorticism was launched publicly, Lewis was 32 years old and one of the oldest members of the group. Gaudier-Brzeska was 23 and Roberts only 19. Lewis was perhaps self-conscious of his age, which might explain why his date of birth in 1882 was, until recently, a mystery. Lewis's art training began at 16 when he won a scholarship to the Slade School and studied there from 1898–1901.

For the next six years he travelled around Europe, living mainly in Paris. Most of his career was spent in England, but he wrote later that, 'my "spiritual home" always has been, if anything, France.'[7] When a schoolboy he had passed some weeks of every year in Paris with his mother, and it was then that he first frequented the galleries. But it was during the years 1902–8 that he seriously studied painting by visiting galleries in Holland, Munich, Madrid and Paris, and copying Old Masters. It was an unproductive period. He published nothing, nor did he exhibit anything during those years, with the exception of one work (lost) in the 1904 New English Art Club exhibition.[8] He wrote later: 'My literary career began in France, in the sense that my first published writings originated in notes made in Brittany. Indeed, this period in retrospect, responsible for much, is a blank with regard to painting.'[9] His friendship and admiration for Augustus John seem also to have stunted his development as a painter. In a letter of c.1908 to his mother he wrote: 'I feel that if I were left alone, I could both write and paint just now: but near John I can never paint, since his artistic personality is just too strong.'[10]

In 1909 his family allowance diminished and he returned to England. Drawings from this date show a hesitant experimental style, combining a number of influences. He was certainly aware of what was happening among the avant-garde painters in Paris. In an unpublished letter to his friend Sturge Moore, he asked if Sturge Moore had managed to 'see any Picasso or Matisse paintings in Paris?'[11] Lewis had also formed an appreciation for primitive art while still a student at the Slade when he made sketches of African masks in the British Museum.[12]

The drawings of 1910 show a gradual simplification of form which becomes harder and more angular in the following year, in drawings like *Smiling Woman Ascending* a Stair (cat.9) and Self-portrait (cat.8). This Cubist faceting of the human forms is taken to a more extreme and exaggerated extent in *The Starry Sky* (cat.20) and *Sunset among the Michelangelos* (cat.22) where the rock-like figures squat motionless on a barren terrain. Already, the blank background of these drawings or the abstract two dimensional forms behind the figure in *Centauress* (cat.10) give the impression of a stage backdrop before which these strange creatures act out their rôles. The theatre was a constant source of inspiration for Lewis, and he makes continual reference to it in his writings. In *Blasting and Bombardiering* he wrote: 'At that period [c.1910] I was an idle student, musing dreams of obstreperous intervention in a farce or two that was going on, upon the stage where the painters acted, and where the aesthetes blinked and blushed.'[13] Augustus John had already observed how much Lewis enjoyed watching the traditional mime and expression of the Commedia dell 'Arte actors in France.[14]

Lewis became more involved with the London art world and from 1911 onwards exhibited with the Camden Town Group, at the Allied Artists' Association and at Roger Fry's Second Post-Impressionist Exhibition. The next important influence on the development of his career appeared with the Exhibition of Works by the Italian Futurists at the Sackville Gallery which exploded on the scene in March, 1912. The notoriety that the Futurists, and particularly Marinetti, achieved through their outspoken propaganda made Lewis realise the importance of publicity. The simultaneous images of the Futurists also had their effect on Lewis's art, producing a splintering and repetition of form as, for example, in the *Timon* series (see cat.26). The initial success of Futurism in England forced Lewis and his associates to analyse and define their own art and to evolve a new and separate style. However, *Blast No. 1* did not appear until June 1914. In July of 1913, a year after the Futurist exhibition, Lewis was befriended by Roger Fry and persuaded to join the Omega Workshops. Work that survives from this period is surprisingly uncharacteristic. *Design for a folding screen* (cat.30) is much more a product of the Bloomsbury Group than that of a budding Vorticist. Lewis was clearly ill at ease in this environment and looked for an excuse to break away, which came with the celebrated Ideal Home rumpus. Lewis, together with Wadsworth, Hamilton and Etchells, left the Omega in October 1913 after accusing Fry of stealing a commission intended for Lewis and Spencer Gore, as well as Fry, in his capacity as director of the Omega Workshops. The commission, by *The Daily Mail*, was to decorate the 'Post-Impressionist Room' at the Ideal Home Exhibition. The subsequent formation of the Rebel Art Centre in 1914 saw the beginning of Lewis's rôle as the rebel, 'the Enemy' of the established Art world. In June, *Blast No. 1* was published.

The magazine's debt to the theatrical propaganda of the Futurists and the anarchic typography of the free-word compositions of Marinetti and Carrà is obvious. The 'Blast' and 'Bless' idea is not original. It is derived from the 'Mer-da' and 'Rose' sections in Apollinaire's 'Futurist Anti-Tradition' Manifesto.[15] Lewis realised the potential impact of an outspoken and provocative manifesto following the example of the Futurists and Apollinaire. He wrote later: 'I planned and launched that hugest and pinkest of all magazines, 'Blast' – whose portentous dimensions, and violent tint did more than would a score of exhibitions to make the public feel that something was happening.'[16] However, Lewis needed to stress the differences between the two movements if his own was to survive. For Lewis, Vorticism was new and distinctive because 'it showed itself more resolute in its exclusion of the past than the Paris School, less concerned with the glittering jazzed-up spectacle of the megalopolis than the Italians, and much more distinct from architecture than the Dutch (such as Mondrian).'[17] It depicted the modern machine age with cool, clear detachment without the sentimentality and emotional fervour of the Futurists – '"Vorticism" accepted the machine-world: that is the point to stress. It sought out machine-forms. The pictures of the Vorticists were a sort of *machines*. This, of course, serves to define Vorticism as the opposite of an "escapist" doctrine. It was cheerfully and dogmatically external.'[18]

The importance of the external appearance of things to Lewis is fundamental to the understanding of his art. 'I am not an anatomist', he wrote, 'I enjoy the surface of life, if not for its own sake, at least not because it conceals the repulsive turbidness of the intestine. Give me the dimple on the cheek of the Gioconda or St John the Baptist, and you can have all the Gothic skeletons or superrealist guts that you like! And what applies to the body applies likewise to the mind. I do not like all these doctors. Give me the surface of the mind, as well. Give me the *outside* of all things, I am a fanatic for the externality of things.'[19] This belief was applied just as strongly to his writings as in, for example, *The Apes of God*. The opposite of the external was the internal view as exemplified in literature by D.H.Lawrence and Joyce, in philosophy by the Bergsonian 'stream of consciousness', and in art by the humanist Greek tradition. 'All our instinctive aesthetic reactions are, in the west of Europe, based upon Greek naturalist canons. Of the *internal* method of approach in literature, Joyce or James are highly representative. Their art (consisting in "telling from the inside", as it is described) has for its background the naturalism (the flowing lines, the absence of linear organization, and also the inveterate humanism) of the Hellenistic pictorial culture.'[20] Vorticism attempted to train people to understand and to appreciate the new external approach as opposed to the internal and, to Lewis, decadent view of art.

If Vorticist art could be equated with any art of the past, it was with what Lewis described as the 'masculine formalism' of the Egyptian and Chinese civilizations. Lewis's description uses another antithetical term – masculine – which is reminiscent of the Futurist glorification of the masculine and contempt for the feminine. This conflict of the opposites occurs throughout his art, his philosophy, and, indeed, his personality. Lewis may appear to be in favour of one view as opposed to its opposite, but he believed that both are essential to the creation of great art. He wrote: 'The painter's especial gift is a much more exquisite, and aristocratic, affair than this female bed of raw emotionality. The two together, if they can only be reconciled, produce the best genius.'[21] This idea of two opposites combining together to produce the best art is also linked with Lewis's belief in the importance of a dual activity. He explained this in a witty journalistic style in *Blast No. 2* when he wrote: 'There is nothing so impressive as the number TWO. You must be a duet in everything. For the individual, the single object, and the isolated, is, you will admit, an absurdity. Why try and give the impression of a consistent and indivisible personality? ... The thought of the old body-and-Soul, Male-and-Female, external duet of existence, can perhaps be of help to you, if you hesitate still to invent yourself properly.'[22] This idea is expressed most clearly in Lewis's art in *Red Duet* (not in exhibition, repr. Cork, p.337) where rows of aggressive shapes confront and intermingle simultaneously. Another aspect of Lewis's dual vision as an artist was the idea of nature *versus* imagination. Looking back on his career, Lewis summarised, 'I have never departed from a dual visual activity. It can really be reduced to what I did when I had nature in front of me, and what I did when I was not making use of nature.'[23]

Many other antithetical concepts relate to Lewis's philosophy of art, such as classic *versus* romantic, rationality *versus* emotion, stasis *versus* flux, the individual *versus* the crowd, war *versus* peace, and, ultimately, death *versus* life. All are opposites but one cannot exist without the other, just as, for Lewis, life cannot exist without art: art is the opposite of life and so art must be equated with death. The much quoted passage in *Tarr* explains this most clearly. Tarr speaks for Lewis when he says: 'Anything living, quick and changing is bad art always ... Deadness is the first condition of art: the second is absence of soul, in the human and sentimental sense. With the statue its lines and masses are its soul, no restless inflammable ego is imagined for its interior: it has *no inside*: good art must have no inside.'[24] All life is continually moving towards death and therefore art, in contrast, should be static and permanent. Lewis expressed this concept more completely as he moved toward pure abstraction in 1914. *Vorticist Composition* (cat.44) of 1915 is a solid mass of rigid forms which fill the picture surface. At this date, Lewis considered Kandinsky to be the only purely abstract painter in Europe, but because he was 'committed, by his theory, to avoid almost all powerful and definite forms', for Lewis, he was 'at the best, wandering and slack.'[25]

The events of the First World War brought about a disillusionment with the pure abstractions of the Vorticist period and Lewis experimented with a semi-abstract, semi-naturalistic style in his work as Official War Artist. His most successful compositions are on a small scale and show a hard and detached vision of the extraordinary events happening around him. His biographical writings of the period, however, give a different picture. Paradoxically, they show an almost Futurist indulgence in, and an unashamedly romantic admiration for, the huge siege guns. 'Out of their throats had sprung a dramatic flame, they had roared, they had moved back. You could see them, lighted from their mouths, as they hurled into the air their great projectiles, and sank back as they did it. In the middle of the monotonous percussion, which had never slackened for a moment, the tom-toming of interminable artillery, for miles around, going on in the darkness ...'[26]

Lewis, embittered by the colossal disruption of the First World War, the waste of four important years and finally, the failure of Group X, went out of public life. He began an intense period of work. He wrote later: 'the obligation to make a new start

– and the decision I took to make a really new start while I was about it – was in the long run beneficial. I might never have submitted myself to the disciplines I did, if I had not been thrown back on myself.'[27] Lewis's reputation as a superb draughtsman rests on the drawings from life of this period. Such a powerful and assured control of line as in *Girl Looking Down* (cat.62), for example, was never to be achieved again. This period, too, saw Lewis's first major oil portraits which were produced in time for the *Tyros and Portraits* exhibition in 1921. The same rigid, sculptural treatment of the human form was worked up into a more sophisticated state of completion in the oils using startling colour contrasts. Lewis is not often regarded as a colourist, but the blue/green tints in the head of *Praxitella* (cat.79) and the red hands and faces of *Tyros reading Ovid* (cat.81) are completely successful. Lewis could not remain out of the limelight for long and the *Tyro No. 1* was published in 1921 under his editorship. The Tyro is a typically grotesque, aggressive and satirical creation and is certainly the kind of public image of himself that Lewis wanted to project. Tyro figures are invariably male and hatted. Lewis was curiously fascinated by flamboyant headwear, frequently sporting a fine example in his many self-portraits. *Self-portrait with Hat* (cat.112) of 1932 is not so far removed from a Tyro mask.

At this date, and throughout his career, Lewis continued to produce semi-abstract, imaginative compositions. *Figure Composition* (cat.81) of 1921 divides the human form into a series of interlocking complex shapes like totem poles. These vertical forms become more abstract in, for example, the three designs done for Olivia Shakespear's dining room and culminating in *Bagdad* (cat.104) of 1927. Titles for Lewis's work are often significant and give clues to the sources in his literary imagination. In a letter to Charles Handley-Read of 1949, Lewis compared his abstract art of the Vorticist period with the imaginative works of the mid 1930s. He wrote: 'Whereas on the musical–abstract (symbols) of 1914 the emotive intellect is let loose (though under some control) upon a multitude of blocks and lines, and composes its fugue: *quite otherwise* in 1935 (or whenever it was) in "The Mud Clinic", [not in exhibition] *the literary imagination* is invited to compose – in a highly selective, but far more complex, world of forms – usually dominated by one colour – say saffron, or blue.'[28]

Lewis was only interested in the new developments in European Art in his rôle as art critic and did not allow them to affect his own work. His own imaginative art depended on literary inspiration. In the late 1920s and 1930s, Lewis experimented with a variety of subject-matter inspired by mythology, historical events and the theme of the after-life paralleled with his three-volume novel *The Human Age*. He enters a dream-world which must owe something to the Surrealist movement, although he was quick to dismiss it when he wrote: 'Surrealism is in effect a sly return to old forms of painting, and not the most desirable at that. That is why I have put it under the heading back-to-nature. It can be described as sly, because it slips back to the plane of the *trompe l'œil* clothed in a highly sensational subject-matter. The subconscious is ransacked to provide the super-realist with an alibi to paint like a Pompier.'[29]

Lewis's artistic career in the 1930s culminated in a large exhibition held at the Leicester Galleries in 1937. From then on, with the exception of a few portraits, his work sees a decline. His disastrous sojourn in America and Canada from 1939–46 produced a further series of pot-boiling portraits. Imaginative work from this period becomes even more fantastic and introspective. For example, *Negro Heaven* (cat.153) of 1946 has more the appearance of an elaborate doodle than a finished drawing.

Lewis's two careers as writer and painter ran concurrently from his student days, but gradually writing claimed the major part of his creative energies. This must have caused considerable conflict. In 1926 he wrote with some bitterness to T.S.Eliot, refusing to write a piece of art criticism for *The Criterion*, adding: 'It may be that as I have not been able for some time to have a studio and practice my delightful calling, that, since I am prevented from doing it, I do not care to *write* about it.'[30] However, although both painting and writing influenced each other, it cannot be said that one became subservient to the other. In fact, it was an uneasy partnership. Lewis wrote: 'From 1924 onwards writing became so much of a major interest that I have tended to work at my painting or drawing in prolonged bursts, rather than fit them into the intervals of the writing or planning of books. Writing and picture-making are not activities, I have found, which mix very well, unless one becomes the servant of the other as was the case with Blake, or with Rossetti.'[31]

The last years spent in London, from his return from America until the onset of blindness, were sad for Lewis the artist. In his most recent autobiography, John Rothenstein wrote: 'when I called on 2 July 1946, at his old studio at 29 Kensington Gardens Studios, Notting Hill Gate, I found him engaged upon a series of portraits, weak in drawing and pallid in colour, which seemed designed merely to flatter. He correctly interpreted my silence as expressive of disapproval, and launched into a justification of flattery, contending that an indigent portrait painter must aim first of all to please his sitters. His arguments were as flimsy as the portraits and as unworthy of his powerful intellect and incisive hand.'[32]

Many people have reacted strongly to Lewis. Often it is an obsessive, uncritical admiration for everything he produced, or at the other extreme, his unfortunate political writings are used as an excuse to ignore his art. Art-historical literature on the modern period stops at Vorticism and, with the exception of a few celebrated portraits, his work is largely ignored. There is no doubt that Vorticism is his chief claim to fame. For once, Britain had produced an artist who, if only for a brief period, was at the forefront of the modern movement. Like so many young artists who reached artistic maturity just before the outbreak of the First World War, he never achieved his full potential. However, the major oils of the 1920s and 1930s, together with a prolific output of drawings and watercolours, leave an *œuvre* of remarkable diversity and originality. At his best, his work can certainly stand up to that of the most celebrated European artists of the first half of this century. It expresses the aggressive force of a penetrating, contradictory, brilliant mind. It is time for a re-assessment of the most neglected of 'The Men of 1914'.

[1] *B & B*. p. 3. Lewis's political views are not discussed in this catalogue. The subject is fully dealt with in G. D. Bridson, *The Filibuster: A Study of the Political Ideas of Wyndham Lewis*, 1972.
[2] *Letters*, p.275
[3] *B & B*, p.88
[4] *B & B*, p.215
[5] *Letters*, pp.212–3
[6] *Letters*, p.274
[7] *Rude Assignment*, p.209
[8] Cork, p.4
[9] *Rude Assignment*, p.113
[10] *Letters*, p.39
[11] Cork, p.11
[12] see cat.3
[13] *B & B*, p.272
[14] Augustus John, *Finishing Touches*, 1964, pp.119–20
[15] Cork, p.249
[16] *Rude Assignment*, p.125
[17] *W L the Artist*, pp.76–77
[18] *W L the Arist*, p.78
[19] *B & B*, p.9
[20] Wyndham Lewis, *Men without Art*, 1934, p.127
[21] *W L the Artist*, p.153–4
[22] Reprinted in *W L the Artist*, pp.204–5
[23] *Rude Assignment*, p.130
[24] Wyndham Lewis, *Tarr* (1st publ. 1918, 2nd edition rewritten 1928), Calder and Boyars: Jupiter Books, 1968, pp. 279–80.
[25] *Blast No. 2*, reprinted in *W L the Artist*, p.140
[26] *B & B*, p.114, quoted in John Rothenstein, *Modern English Painters: Lewis to Moore*, 1956, p.34
[27] *B & B*, p.213
[28] *Letters*, p.505
[29] *W L the Artist*, p.54
[30] *Letters*, p.164
[31] *Rude Assignment*, p.130
[32] John Rothenstein, *Time's Thievish Progress*, 1970, p.35

BLAST First (from politeness) ENGLAND

CURSE ITS CLIMATE FOR ITS SINS AND INFECTIONS

DISMAL SYMBOL, SET round our bodies,
of effeminate lout within.

VICTORIAN VAMPIRE, the LONDON cloud sucks
the TOWN'S heart.

A 1000 MILE LONG, 2 KILOMETER Deep

BODY OF WATER even, is pushed against us
from the Floridas, TO MAKE US MILD.

OFFICIOUS MOUNTAINS keep back DRASTIC WINDS

SO MUCH VAST MACHINERY TO PRODUCE

THE CURATE of "Eltham"
BRITANNIC ÆSTHETE
WILD NATURE CRANK
DOMESTICATED
                    POLICEMAN
LONDON COLISEUM
 SOCIALIST-PLAYWRIGHT
DALY'S MUSICAL COMEDY
GAIETY CHORUS GIRL
TONKS

What was Vorticism?

by Richard Cork

'BLAST First (from politeness) ENGLAND
Curse its climate for its sins and infections
    Dismal symbol, set round our bodies,
        of effeminate lout within.'[1]

With these strident words, some of them printed in gigantic black capitals and arranged on the page like the brashest of vaudeville posters, *Blast No. 1* burst upon London in the summer of 1914 (see illus. opposite). As the opening manifesto from which the above extract is quoted makes abundantly clear, this puce-covered magazine set out to voice an unholy and irreverent impatience with England in general and English art in particular. Wyndham Lewis, who edited *Blast* and wrote most of its manifestos, turned himself into a verbal pugilist. His target was wide, and in the blasting section of the manifestos his typography – which Marshall McLuhan later claimed was set up by an alcoholic printer 'exactly as Lewis required in return for large supplies of liquor'[2] – cursed a succession of besetting maladies.

But *Blast* ridiculed England only because it passionately believed in the country's ability to be purged and turn these weaknesses into strengths. There was a constructive purpose behind the magazine's decision to 'CURSE WITH EXPLETIVE OF WHIRLWIND THE BRITANNIC AESTHETE, CREAM OF THE SNOBBISH EARTH',[3] because such archetypes were to blame for England's desperate shortcomings. And when the English sense of humour came under attack, it too was berated as an obstruction, preventing the nation from treating new ideas with the seriousness they deserved. 'BLAST HUMOUR', screamed the capital letters, 'Quack ENGLISH drug for stupidity and sleepiness. Arch enemy of REAL, conventionalising like gunshot, freezing supple REAL in ferocious chemistry of laughter.'[4]

The most urgent priority of all, however, was to demolish the legacy of the Victorian age which still, in 1914, threatened to stifle any attempt to renew the country and rekindle its creative energies. 'BLAST years 1837 to 1900', cried the manifestos, determined to eradicate the nineteenth century and remind the English that Victorianism was now as irrelevant as the class system it had fostered: 'Curse abysmal inexcusable middle-class (also Aristocracy and Proletariat).'[5] The polemical acrobatics were exhilarating, providing in themselves a model of the high-spirited energy which *Blast No.1* wanted to unleash in the nation it was attacking. England, it insisted, had to shake off its complacent insularity and embrace the full implications of twentieth-century life: only thus could it play a full and vital part in shaping the course of contemporary culture.

Blast No.1 was not simply an anarchic firework, therefore. It was, first and foremost, a serious publication which set out to announce the arrival of a new movement in English art: Vorticism. The list of eleven signatures at the end of the manifesto, including Lawrence Atkinson, Jessica Dismorr, Henri Gaudier-Brzeska, Cuthbert Hamilton, Ezra Pound, William Roberts, Helen Saunders, Edward Wadsworth and Wyndham Lewis himself, proved that this vanguard group was peopled with some of England's most adventurous young artists. And the harsh, combative, undeniably explosive impact of the images they reproduced in *Blast No. 1*'s pages provided an apt visual parallel to the magazine's declaration that 'We are Primitive Mercenaries in the Modern World . . . a movement towards art and imagination could burst up here, from this lump of compressed life, with more force than anywhere else.'[6]

But what sort of movement? Although Vorticism was at pains to point out that 'there is nothing Chauvinistic or picturesquely patriotic about our contentions',[7] it did nevertheless maintain that England had more of a right than any other nation to express the character of the twentieth century in its art. The *Blast* manifestos proudly reminded readers that 'the Modern World is due almost entirely to Anglo-Saxon genius – its appearance and its spirit. Machinery, trains, steam-ships, all that distinguishes externally our time, came far more from here than anywhere else . . . But busy with this LIFE-EFFORT, [England] has been the last to become conscious of the Art that is an organism of this new Order and Will of Man.'[8]

Now, claimed the Vorticists, the time had come. There was no longer any excuse for English art's failure to come to terms with the present and realise that, as *Blast No.1* pointed out, an enormous and challenging new range of unexplored subject-matter was waiting to be employed: 'Our industries, and the Will that determined, face to face with its needs, the direction of the modern world, has reared up steel trees where the green ones were lacking; has exploded in useful growths, and found wilder intricacies than those of Nature.'[9] The words of the manifesto mirror the determination with which the Vorticists viewed this new machine age. Instead of throwing up their hands in horror, like the members of the Royal Academy, and continuing to paint pictures of Roman history or sylvan landscapes as if industrialisation simply did not exist, Lewis and his rebellious compatriots confronted present-day change on its own harsh terms. They saw no point in escaping with Augustus John to a Romany paradise, or even turning their attention with Sickert and the Camden Town Group to the decaying gentility of London street scenes and boarding-house life. How could a Vorticist concentrate on studying the flesh tones of a nude posing on a bed in Mornington Crescent when, as *Blast* insisted, England was busy transforming itself with 'the forms of machinery, Factories, new and vaster buildings, bridges and works'?[10]

The Vorticists had a horror of escapism, and they explained in their manifesto that 'once this consciousness towards the new possibilities of expression in present life has come . . . it will be more the legitimate property of Englishmen than of any other people in Europe. It should also, as it is by origin theirs, inspire them more forcibly and directly. They are the inventors of this bareness and hardness, and should be the great enemies of Romance.'[11] In other words, Vorticism intended to view with deliberate dispassion the subject-matter it had chosen to interpret. It wanted to take upon itself what it saw as the essential character of the machine environment, and become equally dynamic, rigid and implacable. Ezra Pound, who first coined the name 'vortex' and actually christened the movement sometime during the early months of 1914, maintained in *Blast No. 1* that 'the vortex is the point of maximum energy. It represents, in mechanics, the greatest efficiency. We use the words "greatest efficiency" in the precise sense – as they would be used in a text book of MECHANICS.'[12] Pound and his artist allies admired the compressed power of the machine, its ability to perform its function with clean precision and without any messy emotionalism or fuss. They wanted to transfer those attributes to their own art, so that the essence of the machine age which surrounded them could be defined in pictorial and sculptural terms.

One of the most important results of such a programme was that English art approached abstraction for the first time in its development. When *Blast No. 1* explained that 'Machinery is the greatest Earth-medium: incidentally it sweeps away the doctrines of a narrow and pedantic Realism at one stroke',[13] the magazine was indicating how much help the machine had given Vorticism in its struggle to evolve a language which would embody the essence of the contemporary world. None of the Vorticists believed in *total* abstraction, either as a feasible idiom or as an end in itself: the aim was rather to attain a dynamic yet refined vocabulary which replaced literal representation with a richly allusive alternative, full of multi-layered references to the forms of twentieth-century urban life. In *Blast No. 1* Lewis faulted the Italian Futurists for failing to dispense with a banal species of representation: 'With their careful choice of motor omnibuses, cars, lifes, aeroplanes, etc., the Automobilist pictures were too "picturesque", melodramatic and spectacular, besides being undigested and naturalistic to a fault.'[14] Cubism, too, fell into a different but related trap: Lewis declared that Picasso's Cubist sculpture 'no longer so much interprets, as definitely MAKES, nature (and "DEAD" nature at that).'[15]

Although Vorticism owed a profound debt to the combined examples of Cubism and Futurism, it ultimately proved incompatible with both these erstwhile mentors. The Vorticists received much of their initial inspiration from Marinetti's advocacy of machine-age dynamism and the 'beautiful ideas that kill', but they parted company with the Italian movement over how to treat this dynamism in their work. Where the Futurists were unashamedly romantic and rhapsodised about industrial society, expressing their enthusiasm in blurred, multiple imagery, Vorticism was far more coolly appraising about the ambivalent character of twentieth-century change and always affirmed the integrity of the defined, single object.

In this respect, the English movement was closer to Cubism's severe monumentality and planar austerity. But Vorticism could never forgive Picasso and his friends for retaining the old studio motifs in their paintings. Guitars, posed models, and still life on a table-top belonged to the quietist, domesticated art which Vorticism was at pains to reject; and besides, the Cubists combined their preference for traditional, interior subjects with a static sobriety incapable of satisfying the English vanguard's appetite for venomous colour and explosive aggression. The Vorticist ideal was an independent synthesis of Futurism and Cubism, the romantic and the classical, and its desire to control wars with its dynamism so fiercely that a wholly distinctive tension results. The typically diagonal forms of a Vorticist picture thrust outwards, as if the artist is straining to burst the bounds of the picture-frame; but they are contained, even so, by an insistence on precise contours and a solidity of construction which is often sculptural in its implications. Time and again the Vorticist appears to fragment his or her picture-surface to the point of total dispersal, and then recant by locking all its forms together into an inevitable, thoroughly immoveable structure.

Lewis, who along with Pound was the movement's principal theorist, summarised its aims most succinctly when he wrote in 1915 that 'by Vorticism we mean
(a) ACTIVITY as opposed to the tasteful PASSIVITY of Picasso;
(b) SIGNIFICANCE as opposed to the dull or anecdotal character to which the Naturalist is condemned; (c) ESSENTIAL MOVEMENT and ACTIVITY (such as the energy of a mind) as opposed to the imitative cinematography, the fuss and hysterics of the Futurists.'[16] All this was signified by the image of a vortex, a whirling force which would draw together the most vital innovatory energies of the time and crystallise them in a still, rigidly immobile centre. According to Ezra Pound, it was 'a radiant node or cluster . . . from which, and through which, and into which, ideas are constantly rushing.'[17] And Lewis explained his conception of the vortex by telling a friend to think 'at once of a whirlpool . . . At the heart of the whirlpool is a great silent place where all the energy is concentrated. And there, at the point of concentration, is the Vorticist.'[18]

Vorticism saw itself occupying a central, offensive position in the flux of conflicting ideas then circulating among the European avant-garde. London had been exposed to a barrage of these ideas ever since Roger Fry effectively started the bombardment with a notorious exhibition called *Manet and the Post-Impressionists* in the autumn of 1910. The outraged conservative opinion of the English art establishment was only just beginning to recover from the shock when a whole series of invasions followed Fry's initiative. The Futurists arrived in force in March 1912; Fry himself organised the Second Post-Impressionist Exhibition in the autumn of the same year; Severini held a one-man show in April 1913; Brancusi and Kandinsky both caused intense debate at the July 1913 Allied Artists' Salon; and in October 1913 a combined Post-Impressionist and Futurist Exhibition was held. London's younger generation of artists was understandably impressed, and the same relentless pressure was sustained throughout the first half of 1914 with a survey of Modern German Art, a second Futurist Exhibition, and an enormous miscellany at the

Whitechapel Art Gallery called *Twentieth Century Art. A Review of Modern Movements*.

The artists who finally made up the Vorticist movement were on the whole very young: in the spring of 1912, for instance, David Bomberg, William Roberts and Edward Wadsworth were still students at the Slade School of Art. They were bound, therefore, to be dominated for a while by the powerful impact of outside influences; and the London public, who were entertained so consistently by Marinetti's Futurist publicity, came to think of them all as part of the Italian movement. Even when Lewis rallied a number of them around the militant banner of a Rebel Art Centre in March 1914, the misunderstandings continued. And the cross-fire of rivalries came to a climax when Marinetti, with the help of his faithful English disciple Nevinson, issued a special Futurist Manifesto which implied that the rebels were Futurists at heart.

The Rebel Art Centre group did not let this bid pass unchallenged. In a collective letter to the newspapers, they repudiated the Futurist tag which Marinetti and Nevinson had attempted to place on their heads. And although Bomberg added a postscript to make sure that he was not identified as a member of the Rebel Art Centre *either*, the incident did have a crucial effect on the emergent Vorticist movement. For around this time, in early June 1914, Vorticism as an official name first makes its appearance, and within a month *Blast No. 1* arrived to back it up with words and images. At that point, the movement seemed poised to establish itself as a sturdy and long-lived innovatory force in English art, and the overwhelming exuberance of *Blast No. 1* certainly encouraged that hope. 'WE ONLY WANT THE WORLD TO LIVE, and to feel its crude energy flowing through us,' cried the Vorticists, promising to 'convert the King if possible. A VORTICIST KING! WHY NOT? DO YOU THINK LLOYD GEORGE HAS THE VORTEX IN HIM?'[19] Anything seemed possible in the summer of 1914, and *Blast No. 1* was treated for a while as a compulsive talking-point: outrageous, amusing and without a doubt enormously stimulating.

Only a month later, however, the entire situation had altered, irrevocably. In August 1914 the First World War was declared, and cries of military patriotism immediately drowned the expletives of the Vorticists' purely aesthetic call-to-arms. The battleground which they had unconsciously prophesied in so many of their pre-war pictures became an international reality, and most of the Vorticists soon found themselves fighting at the Front rather than waging art combat at home. They were granted little more than a year in which to implement the optimistic proposals outlined in *Blast No. 1* and, considering the paltry time-span they were allotted, their degree of success was surprising. A corpus of work was built up which, while inevitably falling short of both Cubism and Futurism in terms of achievement, did substantiate their claims with a vigour still appreciable today, when well over half of Vorticism's key works are missing.[20] In June 1915 the first Vorticist Exhibition was held in London at the Doré Galleries. And although the list of members printed in the catalogue now contained only seven names – Dismorr, Frederick Etchells,

Gaudier-Brzeska, Lewis, Roberts, Saunders and Wadsworth – most of the rebels were also included in a subsidiary section entitled 'Works By Those Invited To Show'. Atkinson, Bomberg and even the Futurist Nevinson thereby joined forces with the Vorticists in this historic exhibition, while Duncan Grant sent in some abstract assemblage paintings as a reminder that the Bloomsbury artists were reaching a peak of albeit very different audacity during the same period.

Blast No.2, a 'War Number' with a symbolically monochrome cover, was issued a month later to reinforce this display of corporate strength, and even the hostile critic P.G.Konody was forced to admit that the Vorticists demonstrated an 'absolute oneness of purpose and similarity of method'[21] in magazine and exhibition alike. Lewis declared in *Blast No. 2* that 'we have subscribers in the Khyber Pass, and subscribers in Santa Fé. The first stone in the structure of a world-wide reformation of taste has been securely laid.'[22] And if the invigorating high spirits of *Blast No. 1* were now necessarily subdued, to chime with its announcement of Gaudier's tragic death in the trenches, *Blast No. 2* re-affirmed Vorticism's resolve to 'try and brave the waves of blood, for the serious mission it has on the other side of World-War.'[23] British art had been awoken at last to the existence of the first machine age; and machinery's forms – its pistons, cogs, shafts and rods – can be seen articulating all the Vorticists' most radical works. Jacob Epstein, when making his *Rock Drill* sculpture, took this attitude to its logical extreme by actually incorporating a real drill in his work of art. But most Vorticist pictures operate more tangentially than that, letting machinery aid them in terms of organisation and ruling principles when it came to finalising their metaphors of the new century.

The awkward fact remained, however, that not one single review of the Vorticist Exhibition could be described as at all favourable. Without the support of their former champion, the critic and philosopher T.E.Hulme, the Vorticists were treated as an incomprehensible joke. Such a reception must have been severely discouraging to the rebels, whose inability to find support of any kind was compounded when active service in the army absorbed the residue of their energies in 1916. The tireless Ezra Pound continued to propagate the Vorticist cause with typical generosity throughout the war, publishing a heartfelt *Memoir* of his close friend Gaudier, encouraging Alvin Langdon Coburn to experiment with his photographic Vortography, and then persuading the American collector John Quinn to purchase Vorticist work on an extensive scale. Quinn even opened an Exhibition of the Vorticists in New York on 10 January 1917, when 75 paintings and drawings by Dismorr, Etchells, Lewis, Roberts, Saunders and Wadsworth were shown at the Penguin Club, 8 East 15th Street, an artists' society recently founded by Walt Kuhn and a number of his friends. But the general reaction to this under-publicised and absurdly retrospective sample was disappointingly similar to the reception accorded to *Blast No. 1* by the *New York Times* in 1914: 'What is Vorticism? . . . It is the reductio ad absurdum of mad modernity.'[24]

Nothing, ultimately, could overcome the disastrous vacuum created by the Vorticists' prolonged absence at the front line of war. And when they all returned in

1918, the movement no longer existed. Sickened by the realisation that the machines which had once inspired them could cause untold human misery, the former rebels turned their back on radicalism and in their various ways returned to a more representational style. Lewis made a half-hearted attempt to rally them again for a third issue of *Blast* in 1919, but it was doomed to remain unpublished: the whole heady context of pre-war London, which provided such an ideal environment for the fermentation of experimental ideas, had vanished for ever. Within a few years Vorticism was virtually forgotten, and only today is it coming to be seen as a stimulating attempt to blast a parochial, backward-looking culture into realising that, as the rebels' manifesto asserted, 'an Art must be organic with its Time.'[25] Now, over 60 years later, we can appreciate how the oppositional extremism of Vorticism's standpoint condemned it to an isolated place on the outer edges of the society it hoped to affect. But at a time when increasing efforts are being made to replace the avant-garde tradition with a more socially integrated alternative, the Vorticist adventure still holds good for its determination to forge an art capable of making its audience keenly aware of the condition of the modern world.

[1] *Blast No. 1*, London 1914, p.11
[2] Marshall McLuhan, *Counterblast*, London 1970 edition, p. 5. *Counterblast* is openly inspired by the example of *Blast No. 1*
[3] *Blast No. 1*, p.15
[4] Ibid., p.17
[5] Ibid., p.18
[6] Ibid., pp.30,32
[7] Ibid., p.34
[8] Ibid., p.39
[9] Ibid., p.36
[10] Ibid., p.40
[11] Ibid., p.41
[12] Ezra Pound, 'Vortex. Pound', ibid., p.153
[13] Ibid., p.39
[14] Wyndham Lewis, 'The Melodrama of Modernity', ibid., p. 144
[15] Wyndham Lewis, 'Relativism and Picasso's Latest Work', ibid., p. 140
[16] Wyndham Lewis, 'Note' to the catalogue of 'The First Exhibition of the Vorticist Group, opening 10th June 1915, at the Doré Galleries, London'
[17] Ezra Pound, 'Vorticism', *Fortnightly Review*, 1 September 1914
[18] Douglas Goldring, *South Lodge*, London 1943, p.65
[19] 'Long Live the Vortex', *Blast No. 1*, unpaginated
[20] For example: 38 of the 49 works shown by the full members of the movement at the 1915 Vorticist Exhibition are now missing. The majority of them entered the John Quinn collection and were sold after his death (see the sale catalogue, *Paintings and Sculptures. The Renowned Collection of Modern and Ultra-Modern Art, Formed by the Late John Quinn*, New York 1927.)
[21] P. G. Konody, *The Observer*, 4 July 1915
[22] Wyndham Lewis, 'Notice To Public', *Blast No. 2*, London 1915, p.7
[23] Wyndham Lewis, 'Editorial', *Blast No. 2*, p.5
[24] *New York Times*, 9 August 1914
[25] *Blast No. 1*, p.34

Wyndham: an appreciation

by Omar S. Pound

'What kind of hat is she wearing?' 'Is she ugly?', asked a clear voice across a breakfast-table in the small dining-room on the ferry from Fishguard to Cork – an embarrassing but illuminating insight into reality for a young man. Wyndham, who was almost totally blind when I took him to Ireland in 1951, insisted on me describing everything to him – not for his personal safety but because he was interested, wanted to know, and was ever afraid someone might try to keep something from him. Despite his blindness Lewis retained visual acuity right to the end, as any reader of *The Human Age* knows.

After the horrors of the First World War, instead of retreating pusillanimously into Dada and the Abstract, he rushed lustily into drawing and painting people and developing his stimulating imaginary world as a humanist metaphysician, and throughout the 1920s and 1930s he produced some of the most interesting British portraits of the twentieth century – interesting perhaps because Lewis never flattered a sitter.

Right to the end two constant passions emanated from him, through his paintings and writings: people (and therefore politics) and the metaphysical world.

This exhibition is evidence that appreciation of his imagination and visual integrity is still growing.

Selected Bibliography

The abbreviations are those used for references in the text.

Michel   Walter Michel, *Wyndham Lewis: Paintings and Drawings*, London, Thames and Hudson, 1971. Each catalogue entry has a reference to Walter Michel's catalogue raisonné, and particular acknowledgement should be made to this pioneering work.

Charles Handley-Read, *The Art of Wyndham Lewis*, London, Faber and Faber, 1951.

Letters   W.K.Rose (ed.), *The Letters of Wyndham Lewis*, London, Methuen, 1963.

Walter Michel and C.J.Fox (eds), *Wyndham Lewis on Art*, London, Thames and Hudson, 1971.

Geoffrey Wagner, *Wyndham Lewis, a Portrait of the Artist as The Enemy*, London, Routledge and Kegan Paul, 1957.

Cork   Richard Cork, *Vorticism and Abstract Art in the First Machine Age*, London, Gordon Fraser, 1976.

Sir John Rothenstein, 'Wyndham Lewis', in *Modern English Painters: Lewis to Moore*, London, Eyre & Spottiswoode, 1956.

Sir John Rothenstein, *Wyndham Lewis and Vorticism*. Exhibition catalogue, London, the Tate Gallery, 1956.

Anthony D'Offay, *Abstract Art in England 1913–15*. Exhibition catalogue, London, 1969.

Jeffrey Meyers, *The Enemy. A Biography of Wyndham Lewis*, London, Routledge & Kegan Paul, 1980.

Books by Lewis

B & B   *Blasting and Bombardiering*, London, Eyre and Spottiswoode, 1937. 2nd edition, London, Calder and Boyars, 1967 (references in the text refer to this edition).

Wyndham Lewis the Artist, from 'Blast' to Burlington House, London, Laidlow and Laidlow, 1939.

Rude Assignment, a Narrative of My Career Up-to-Date, London, Hutchinson, 1950.

Tarr, London, The Egoist Press, 1918; revised and rewritten edition, London, Chatto and Windus, 1928; Pelham Library edition, Chatto and Windus, 1941; London, Methuen, 1951; London, Calder and Boyars: Jupiter Books, 1968.

The Wild Body: A Soldier of Humour and Other Stories, London, Chatto and Windus, 1927.

Men Without Art, London, Cassell, 1934.

The Human Age (3 vols), London, Methuen, 1955–6; 2nd edition, London, John Calder, 1965–6.

Magazines edited by Lewis

Blast. Review of the Great English Vortex, London, John Lane, The Bodley Head: *No.1*, 20 June 1914; *No.2*, 2 July 1915. Reprinted, London, Frank Cass, and New York, Kraus Reprint, both 1968.

The Tyro, a Review of the Arts of Painting, Sculpture and Design, London, The Egoist Press: *No.1*, 1921; *No.2*, 1922. Reprinted, London, Frank Cass, 1970.

The Enemy, a Review of Art and Literature, London, The Arthur Press: *Nos.1 and 2*, 1927; *No.3*, 1929. Reprinted, London, Frank Cass, 1968.

For bibliographies on Lewis's writings, see:

Omar S. Pound and Philip Grover, *Wyndham Lewis: A Descriptive Bibliography*, Folkestone, Dawson: Archon Books, 1978.

Bradford Morrow and Bernard Lafourcade, *A Bibliography of the Writings of Wyndham Lewis*, Santa Barbara, Black Sparrow Press, 1978.

Chronology

1882   18 November: Lewis born on his father's yacht moored near Amherst, Nova Scotia, Canada. Son of an American, Charles E. Lewis, and his English wife, Anne Stuart Prickett.

1893   His parents separate and Lewis lives with his mother in the suburbs of London. Educated at a number of public schools, finishing at Rugby which he left in 1898 at the age of 16.

1898–1901   A student at the Slade School. His literary talents encouraged by a group of men working at the British Museum, including T. Sturge Moore, R. A. Streatfield and Laurence Binyon.

c.1902–8   Travelling on the Continent, living mainly in Paris, but visiting Germany, Holland and Spain. He remained for six months at the Heimann Academy in Munich and shared a studio with Spencer Gore in Madrid c.1902. He spent much time with Augustus John in Paris and during the summer months in Brittany, on one occasion in the company of Henry Lamb. In Paris, he attended Bergson's lectures and was associated with the extreme right wing of Action Française.

1904   Exhibits one work *Study of a Girl's Head* (lost) at the New English Art Club.

1909   Allowance diminishes and he returns to England. First stories published in Ford Madox Hueffer's *English Review*. Meets Ezra Pound.

1910   Douglas Goldring publishes some of Lewis's stories and a poem in *The Tramp*.

1911   June: exhibits *The Architect No.1* and *No.2* at the first exhibition of the Camden Town Group at the Carfax Gallery, Oxford. December: exhibits *Port de Mer*, *Au Marché*, *Virgin and Child* at second Camden Town Group exhibition.

1912   Meets Roger Fry. May: included in the exhibition of contemporary British art at the Galerie Barbazanges, Paris, selected by Fry. Madame Strindberg commissions Lewis and others to decorate her Cabaret Theatre Club which opens 26 June. July: exhibits *Creation* at the Fifth Exhibition of the Allied Artists' Association. October: exhibits *Creation* and eight drawings, including some of the *Timon* drawings, in Roger Fry's Second Post-Impressionist Exhibition at the Grafton Galleries. December: exhibits *Dance* at the third Camden Town Group exhibition at the Carfax Gallery. Meets Bomberg.

1913   July: exhibits three works, including *Group* at the Sixth Allied Artists' Association Exhibition. Exhibits at First Grafton Group Exhibition. Joins Omega Workshops opened by Roger Fry, later joined by Wadsworth, Hamilton, Etchells, Bomberg and Roberts. 5 October: leaves workshop after row with Fry over Ideal Home Exhibition. The 'Round Robin' signed by Lewis, Etchells, Hamilton and Wadsworth sent to the press. October: exhibits seven works at Frank Rutter's Post-Impressionist and Futurist Exhibition at the Doré Galleries, including *Creation* and *Kermesse*. November: a dinner organised in

Marinetti's honour by Etchells, Hamilton, Lewis, Nevinson and Wadsworth. Commissioned to decorate Lady Drogheda's dining room. December: exhibits at Camden Town Group show at Brighton and writes a foreword in the catalogue to 'The Cubist Room'. *Timon of Athens* portfolio published by the Cube Press.

1914   March: the Rebel Art Centre founded at 38 Great Ormond Street. Lewis exhibits five works at the first London Group exhibition at the Goupil Gallery, including *Christopher Columbus*, *Eisteddfod*, *Enemy of the Stars* and *Ezra Pound*. June: exhibits *Slow Attack* at the Twentieth Century Art Exhibition at the Whitechapel Art Gallery. 20 June: *Blast No.1* published. July: exhibited *Night Attack* and *Signalling* at the Allied Artists' Association Salon.

1915   March: exhibits *The Crowd* and *Workshop* at the second London Group exhibition. Commissioned to decorate dining room of the Restaurant de la Tour Eiffel. June: exhibits four paintings, including *Red Duet* and *Workshop*, and six woodcuts. 2 July: *Blast No.2* published.

1916   March: Lewis enlists in the Garrison Artillery. Period of training in a succession of English artillery camps first as a Gunner then as a Bombardier. Towards the end of 1916, gained admission to the Cadet Artillery School at Exeter.

1917   January: participates in the Vorticist Exhibition at the Penguin Club, New York. End of May: leaves for Western Front as a subaltern in a Siege Battery. December: seconded as a war artist to the Canadian Corps Headquarters at Vimy Ridge and commissioned to paint a picture for the Canadian War Memorials Fund (*A Canadian Gun Pit*, National Gallery of Canada, Ottawa).

1918   Publication of *Tarr* (written during the winter of 1914/15). Commissioned to paint a picture by the Imperial War Museum (*A Battery Shelled*).

1919   February: first one-man exhibition, *Guns*, at the Goupil Gallery. October: *The Caliph's Design: Architects! Where is Your Vortex?* published.

1920   March–April: organises Group X Exhibition at the Mansard Gallery, exhibiting seven self-portraits.

1921   April: *The Tyro No.1* published. Second one-man show, *Tyros and Portraits*, held at the Leicester Galleries. September: visits Berlin.

1922   March: *The Tyro No.2* published. October: visits Venice as a guest of Nancy Cunard.

1922–5   A period of retirement from public life, mainly spent in writing.

1926   March: Lewis's first political polemic, *The Art of Being Ruled*, published. September: visits Spain.

1927   January: *The Enemy No.1* – a review of art and literature – published. September: *Time and Western Man* published. Visited New York several times during this period.

1928   June: *The Childermass* published, the first part of a projected trilogy. September: *The Enemy No.2* published. December: a revised edition of *Tarr* published.

1929   September: *The Enemy No.3* published.

1930   June: *The Apes of God* published. 9 October: marries Gladys Anne Hoskyns. November: visits Germany.

1931   Visits Morocco and other parts of North Africa in the late spring. December: visits America.

1932   September: visits Germany. October: exhibition *Thirty Personalities* held at the Lefevre Galleries. November: portfolio *Thirty Personalities and a Self-Portrait* published by Desmond Harmsworth.

1932–7 Seriously ill as a result of a gland infection contracted in the First World War, necessitating a number of operations and periods of convalescence. Three of his books are withdrawn, either before or after publication.

1937   October: published *Blasting and Bombardiering*. December: a large exhibition of paintings and drawings held at the Redfern Gallery.

1938   May: the rejection of the portrait of T.S.Eliot by the Royal Academy selection committee, followed by Augustus John's resignation in protest. July: a one-man show at the Beaux-Arts Gallery.

1939   June: *Wyndham Lewis the Artist: from 'Blast' to Burlington House* published.

1939–45 Spent in USA and Canada. Stayed at New York City, Buffalo and Windsor, Ontario. In November 1940 moved to Toronto where he remained until June 1943. Exhibited at the Duncan Gallery, Toronto. Accepted a year's lectureship at Assumption College, Windsor, Ontario where he remained until May 1945. August: returned to London.

1946   Appointed art critic to *The Listener* magazine.

1949   May: retrospective exhibition at the Redfern Gallery.

1950   February: exhibition of watercolours at Victoria College, Toronto. November: published *Rude Assignment: A narrative of my career up-to-date*.

1951   10 May: announces loss of his sight in *The Listener*. Awarded a Civil List pension.

1952   Awarded an honorary Litt.D. by Leeds University.

1954   November: publishes *The Demon of Progress in the Arts* – an attack on extremism in the visual arts.

1955   His trilogy *The Human Age* broadcast on the Third Programme of the BBC. The first part, *The Childermass*, published in 1928; the sequels *Monstre Gai* and *Malign Fiesta* were commissioned by the BBC in 1951.

1956   Retrospective exhibition at the Tate Gallery organised by Sir John Rothenstein.

1957   Died on 7 March in London.

Note to catalogue

Drawings are on white paper unless
otherwise stated.

Measurements: in inches height before
width, followed by centimetres.

Coll: Previous Collection.

Books, pamphlets and magazines are not
included. For a complete catalogue of
Lewis's writings, see the two recently
published bibliographies listed in the
Selected Bibliography p. 41.

Each entry has a reference to Walter
Michel's catalogue raisonné – see the
Selected Bibliography p. 41.

1

2

3

Lewis became a student at the Slade School in 1898, at the age of 16, after an undistinguished education at a number of public schools. The first important influence on his developing career was provided by the overpowering personality of Augustus John. John had left the Slade in that year, but its walls still 'bore witness to the triumphs of this "Michelangelo" '.

1

Nude Boy Bending Over

1900
Black chalk
$13\frac{1}{2} \times 11\frac{1}{2}$ (34·5 × 29)
Inscribed (in another hand): *P.W.Lewis. Scholarship 1900*
Michel (2)

A sensitive nude study which enabled Lewis to win a Slade scholarship competition in 1900. It follows the academic tradition of draughtsmanship of which Professor Tonks would have approved but, in particular, it shows the influence of Augustus John's Rembrandtesque life drawings. In *Rude Assignment*, Lewis describes a visit by John to the life-class at the Slade in which John produced a number of sketches of the model which were not in the 'grand manner' favoured by Tonks, but appeared to have come 'out of the workshop of Rembrandt van Rhyn.'[1]

[1] Wyndham Lewis, *Rude Assignment*, 1950, p.119
Slade School of Fine Art, University College, London

The years c.1902–8 were spent travelling on the Continent, living mainly in Paris. Lewis had a studio there and also studied at the Heimann Academy in Munich, but no work survives from this period. From c.1909–17, a more complete group of drawings remains, largely as a result of Lewis's friendship with Captain Lionel Guy Baker, who died at the end of the First World War. Lewis remembers him with affection in *Blasting and Bombardiering*. Captain Baker bequeathed twenty-seven drawings by Lewis to the Victoria and Albert Museum.

2

Anthony

c.1909
Pen and ink, gouache
$5\frac{5}{8} \times 4\frac{1}{2}$ (14·5 × 11·5)
Unsigned
Coll: Capt. Lionel Guy Baker
Michel (11)

Possibly one of two drawings exhibited at the Camden Town Group exhibition of June 1911. Neither exhibit has been positively identified but *Architect with Green Tie* (Michel 12, not in exhibition) corresponds closely to a visitor's description.[1] *Anthony* has the same ink cross-hatching with the head sharply outlined against a blank background. The head clearly shows Lewis's interest in primitive Oceanic maskheads (see cat.3) and also German Expressionism (see cat.45). However, the upturned nose and smiling expression add a comic note. Richard Cork's quotation from 'The Pole' (a short story by Lewis published in 1909) could perhaps be more aptly applied to *Anthony*, in particular the lines: 'In his rigid and absorbed manner, with his smiling mask, he looked as though a camera's recording and unlidded eye were in front of him, and if he stirred or his expression took another tone, the spell would be broken, the plate blurred, his chance lost.'[2] The title is probably inspired by Shakespeare's characterization of Mark Anthony (see cat.3).

[1] Cork, pp.14–15
[2] ibid., p.15
Victoria and Albert Museum (E. 3778–1919)

3

The Theatre Manager

1909
Pen and ink, watercolour
$11\frac{5}{8} \times 12\frac{3}{8}$ (29·5 × 31·5)
Signed: *W.Lewis. / 1909.*
Coll: Capt. Lionel Guy Baker
Michel (15)

One of the earliest examples of Lewis's life-long fascination for the stage and actors. A muddled composition which shows the young artist experimenting with a mixture of styles. Richard Cork has pointed out that the nude recalls a figure in Dürer's engraving *The Four Witches*, and the profile in the middle background is reminiscent of Leonardo's grotesques.[1] As in *Anthony* (see cat.2), the mask-like heads show an awareness of primitive art which Lewis began to study whilst undergoing the more traditional training at the Slade. In 1947, he wrote to James Thrall Soby, 'In an early sketchbook the other day full of Leonardo's old man with the swollen underlip and Michelangelo's writhing heavyweights I

came across Pacific Island masks.'[2]
It has been suggested that *The Theatre Manager* is one of the first pictures by a British artist to show the impact of Picasso's *Les Demoiselles d'Avignon* of 1907. Augustus John had seen the picture in Picasso's studio, but it is not clear whether Lewis saw it himself.[3] The image reflected in the mirror bears a close resemblance to the likeness of Shakespeare. In his book *The Lion and the Fox. The rôle of the hero in the plays of Shakespeare* (1927), Lewis saw Shakespeare as 'the perfect *mirror* of the advice to the players in *Hamlet*, he is one of the star exemplars of art's self-effacing aloofness. His, too, is the infinitely supple mind; to his blank and non-committal countenance you could truly say, "Your wit is of the true Pierian spring / That can make anything of anything" . . .'[4]
A passage in Gustave Le Bon's influential book *The Crowd. A Study of the Popular Mind* (first published in English in 1896) may also be relevant to *The Theatre Manager*. Le Bon wrote: 'It is often impossible on reading plays to explain their success. Managers of theatres when accepting pieces are themselves, as a rule, very uncertain of their success, because to judge that matter it would be necessary that they should be able to transform themselves into a crowd.'[5]

[1] Cork, p.10
[2] *Letters*, p.407
[3] Cork, pp.10–11
[4] W.Lewis, *The Lion and the Fox*, 1927, p.13
[5] Gustave Le Bon, *The Crowd. A study of the Popular Mind*, edition published 1913, p.58. I am indebted to Chris Mullen for pointing out the connections between Lewis and Gustave Le Bon.

Victoria and Albert Museum (E. 3779–1919)

4

Dieppe Fishermen

1910
Pen and ink
$10\frac{3}{4} \times 8\frac{3}{8}$ (27·5 × 21·5)
Signed: *Wyndham Lewis 1910.*
Coll: Agnes Bedford
Michel (19)

The subject-matter, together with the simplified forms of the burly sailors and the rhythmic use of line, show the influence of Matisse, for example, *Young Sailor 1* of 1906. The subject-matter can also be compared with Lewis's short stories written before the First World War which were re-

4

published in 1927 under the title *The Wild Body*. Many derive their inspiration from the Breton peasant community. There are frequent references in the text to the rolling gait of the menfolk, for example, in 'Beau Sejour' one of the central characters is described stamping 'heavily out into the garden in his sabots, rolling, husky peasant fashion, from side to side.'[1]

[1] W.Lewis, *The Wild Body: A Soldier of Humour and other stories*, 1927, p.75

Private Collection

5 see colour plate I

Odalisque

c.1911–12
Pen and ink, chalk
12 × 7 (30·5 × 17·8)
Unsigned
Coll: Dorothy Pound
Michel (?79)

A powerful image in which the figure's erotic charms and flamboyant pose are contrasted with the expressionless mask. The subject-matter is probably inspired by Matisse. The date is uncertain. It is closest stylistically to Lewis's design for the Cabaret Theatre Club poster of 1912 (Michel 40) and *The Dancers*, 1912 (cat.14A), but the tighter use of line suggests that it was begun slightly earlier.

Private Collection

6

Mamie

1911
Pencil and wash
$11 \times 10\frac{1}{4}$ (28 × 26)
Signed: *Wyndham Lewis 1911.*
Coll: John Quinn; A. Conger Goodyear
Michel (23)

An early study from life which shows a markedly harder faceting of form and an awareness of analytical Cubism. The same model posed for *Girl Asleep* (see cat.7).

With Ivor Braka, London

7

Girl Asleep

1911
Pencil and brown wash
$11 \times 15\frac{1}{4}$ (28 × 38·5)
Signed: *Wyndham Lewis. 1911.*
Coll: Charles Rutherston
Michel (21)

A confident and assured work in which Lewis has successfully assimilated the Cubist style to combine bold outline with delicate shading.

City of Manchester Art Galleries (1925.504)

8

Self-portrait

c.1911–12
Pencil and watercolour
$12 \times 9\frac{1}{2}$ (30·5 × 23·5)
Signed: *W.Lewis*
Coll: Mrs Anne Wyndham Lewis
Michel (26)

One of a series of three pencil self-portraits done at this date (see Michel 24–26, No.25, repr. Cork, p.84). All three drawings are expressions of the aggressive and threatening public image that Lewis wanted to project.

C. J. Fox

9

Smiling Woman Ascending a Stair

1911–12
Charcoal, watercolour and gouache
$37\frac{1}{2} \times 25\frac{1}{2}$ (95 × 65)
Signed: *Wyndham Lewis*
Michel (27)

A study for the painting *The Laughing Woman* (destroyed) for which Kate Lechmere remembers posing.[1] An interview with Lewis was published in *The Daily News and Leader* on 7 April 1914 in which Lewis is quoted as saying about the work: 'That

6

picture is a Laugh though rather a staid and traditional explosion. The body is a pedestal for the laugh. Although the forms of the figure and head perhaps look rather unlikely to you, they are more or less accurate, as representation. It was done from life.'

Laughter was, for Lewis, one of the most interesting and revealing of emotions. In his book *Men Without Art*, Lewis wrote: 'Laughter – humour and wit – has a function in relation to our tender consciousness; a function similar to that of art. It is the preserver much more than the destroyer. And, in a sense, *everyone* should be laughed at or else *no one* should be laughed at. It seems that ultimately that is the alternative.'[2] Of the characters in one of *The Wild Body* stories, Lewis wrote: 'Their laughter is sharp and mirthless and designed usually to wound. With their grins and quips they are like armed men who never meet without clashing their weapons together.'[3]

Richard Cork makes an interesting comparison with Augustus John's *Smiling Woman* of c.1909 and suggests that Lewis may be mocking a work by his former hero.[4]

The title recalls Duchamp's famous *Nude Descending a Staircase*, first shown at the Salon des Indépendants in February 1912. The picture may have had an indirect influence on Lewis. Like Lewis, Duchamp viewed his subjects with a cold, satirical eye and equated the human body with machines. However, unlike *Smiling Woman Ascending a Stair*, Duchamp's picture is concerned with rendering a figure in successive stages of motion.

[1] Cork, p.146
[2] W.Lewis, *Men Without Art*, 1934, p.109
[3] W.Lewis, *The Wild Body*, 1927, p.160
[4] Cork, pp.19–20

The Vint Trust

10

Centauress

1912
Pen and ink, wash
$12\frac{1}{8} \times 14\frac{1}{2}$ (31 × 37)
Signed: *Wyndham Lewis. 1912.*
Coll: John Quinn; Richard Wyndham; Charles Handley-Read
Michel (41)

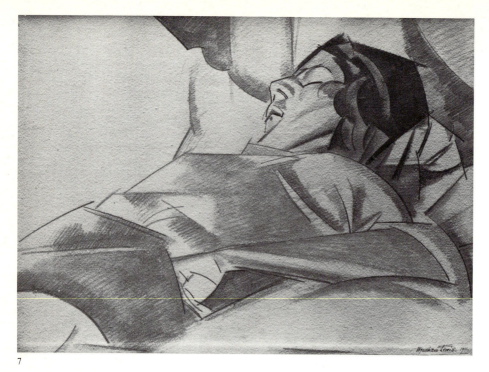

7

8

10

9

11

A fragile mythological creature confronted by the harsh and threatening forms of the modern industrial world. The forms are awkward and unresolved, but nevertheless, the design has considerable power.

The Trustees, the Cecil Higgins Art Gallery, Bedford

11

The Courtesan

1912
Pen and ink, pastel
$10\frac{3}{4} \times 7\frac{1}{4}$ (27·5 × 18·5)
Signed: *W Lewis. 1912*
Coll: Capt. Lionel Guy Baker
Michel (44)

A sophisticated design which, as in Futurist painting, loses some of its force because of the stress on the literary content. The timeless scene of a procuress whispering into a courtesan's ear is transformed into a defiantly Vorticist image.

Victoria and Albert Museum (E.3761–1919)

12

Courtship

1912
Pen and ink, chalk
$10\frac{1}{8} \times 8\frac{1}{8}$ (25·5 × 20·5)
Signed: *W.L. 1912.*
Coll: Capt. Lionel Guy Baker
Michel (45)

12

One of a series of pen drawings of pin-head figures strutting about in an anonymous landscape performing their own instinctive rituals. In contrast to *The Courtesan* (cat.11), Lewis has deliberately removed all the distracting details of costume, background and facial expression so that the eye concentrates on the figures' ungainly movements. This series can be closely paralleled with *The Wild Body* stories where the characters act out the repetitive rituals of their daily lives. In *Bestre*, Lewis describes the confrontation of two figures as 'a matter of who could be most silent and move least: it was a stark stand-up fight between one personality and another,

53

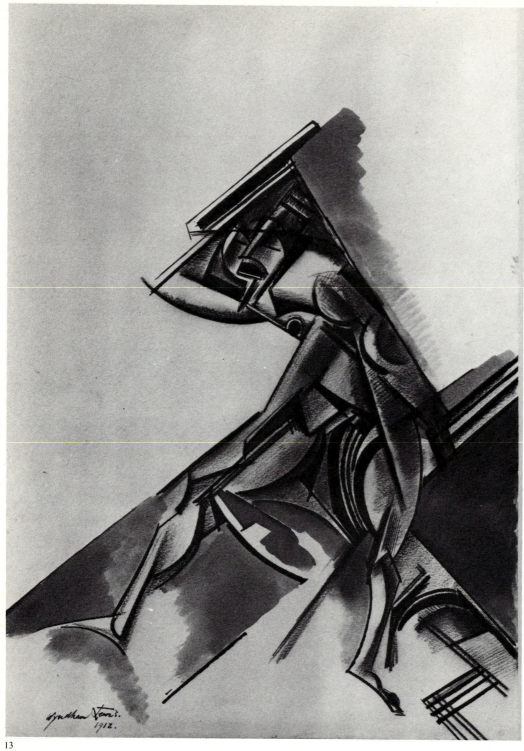

13

unaided by adventitious muscle or tongue. It was more like phases of a combat or courtship in the insect-world.'[1]

[1] W.Lewis, *The Wild Body*, 1927, p.126

Victoria and Albert Museum (E.3785–1919)

13

The Vorticist

1912
Pen and ink, watercolour
$16\frac{1}{2} \times 12$ (42 × 30·5)
Signed: *Wyndham Lewis. 1912.*
Coll: Edward Wadsworth; Denys Sutton
Michel (118)

One of the most successful drawings from this period in the style of *The Courtesan* (see cat.11) which combines the complexity of form of analytical Cubism with the dynamism of the Futurists. As Richard Cork points out, the pose, gesture and facial expression are strikingly reminiscent of the type of actor-warriors that appear on Japanese prints.[1] The title was given at a later date, perhaps by Wadsworth, its former owner.

[1] Cork, p.31

Southampton Art Gallery

14A

The Dancers (Study for Kermesse?)

1912
Pen and black ink, watercolour, gouache on buff paper
$11\frac{3}{4} \times 11\frac{1}{2}$ (29·5 × 29)
Signed: *WL* and *Wyndham Lewis. 1912.*
Coll: John Quinn; Richard Wyndham; Ivan Phillips
Michel (48)

A powerful and sophisticated design which appears to be a development from *Design for a programme cover – Kermesse* (cat.14) and the wash drawing *Kermesse* of 1912 (Michel 72, repr. Cork p.40). The number of figures is reduced and all distracting details of costume and facial expression are removed. The stylization of the head recalls *Odalisque* (cat.5). Judging by contemporary reviews of cat.14) the final oil painting, which also contained three figures, was more stylized and unrepresentational. Clive Bell recommended that the viewer should 'shed all irrelevant prejudices in favour of representation' in order to appreciate *Kermesse* 'as a piece of pure design.'[1]

[1] Review by Clive Bell in *The Athenaeum*, 27 July 1912, see Cork p.42.

With the Mayor Gallery, London

14A

Design for a programme cover – Kermesse

1912
Pen and ink
$11\frac{1}{4} \times 12\frac{1}{4}$ (28·5 × 31)
Signed: *WL 1912*
Coll: John Quinn; R.Wyndham
Michel (52)

A study probably connected with the large oil entitled *Creation* (lost) exhibited at the Allied Artists' Association summer salon in 1912. Roger Fry noted in his review of the exhibition that *Creation* was a 'design of a Kermesse, originally intended for the Cave of the Calf, the new Cabaret Theatre.'[1] The

picture seems to have subsequently been given the title *Kermesse* – an annual fair or carnival characterized by much noisy merry-making. It measured 8′ 9″ × 8′ 11″, and some idea of its appearance can be obtained from Horace Brodzky's etching *Viewing Kermesse* (cat.156) done when the picture was exhibited at the Penguin Club, New York in 1917.

Madame Strindberg commissioned Lewis to decorate her nightclub 'The Cave of the Golden Calf', later known as 'The Cabaret Theatre Club' in 1912. The title of this watercolour suggests that Madame

14

15

16

Strindberg commissioned it for one of the Club's publicity leaflets. The mask-like faces of the men leer menacingly at the central figure of the woman who struggles to escape from their grasp. The men appear to be wearing the broad-brimmed black hats of the Breton peasants. The position of the heads and the curving forms create a Futurist whirl.

[1] see Cork, p.37

Private Collection

15

The Domino

1912
Pen and ink, watercolour
$10 \times 8\frac{1}{8}$ (25·5 × 20·5)
Signed: *WL. 1912.*
Coll: Capt. Lionel Guy Baker
Michel (54)

Similar to *Courtship* (see cat.12), the hesitant pen line shows Lewis experimenting with a simplification and distortion of the human form. The elegant poses resemble the movement of dancers. They gesture towards the domino – a loose cloak accompanied by a mask traditionally worn at masquerades.

Victoria and Albert Museum (E.3784–1919)

16

Indian Dance

1912
Black chalk and watercolour
$10\frac{3}{4} \times 11\frac{1}{2}$ (27 × 29)
Signed: *Wyndham Lewis 1912.*
Coll: Richard Wyndham
Michel (69)

The figures, absorbed in their own movements, act out their primitive dance ritual under a harsh bright light like a stage spot. Lewis's debt to primitive sculpture is clear. He may also have been indirectly influenced by the impact of the Diaghilev Ballet, for example, the angular, awkward dance movements of the Polovtsian dances from *Prince Igor*, premiered in Paris in May 1909 and in England in June 1911.

The Trustees of the Tate Gallery (6257)

17

Lovers

1912
Pen and ink, watercolour
10×14 (25·5 × 35·5)
Signed: *Wyndham Lewis. 1912.*
Coll: Sir Osbert Sitwell
Michel (74)

A powerful composition where the ecstatic emotions of the entwined couples are conveyed by the swirling abstract shapes around them, reminiscent of Futurist lines of force. It relates to the series of studies associated with *Kermesse* (see cat.14). The design of interlocking arcs may also owe a debt to Kupka's work of this date and particularly his *Amorpha*, exhibited at the Salon d'Automne in 1912.

Private Collection

18

Russian Scene

1912
Pen and ink, chalk, watercolour
$12 \times 9\frac{1}{2}$ (30·5 × 24)
Signed: *Wyndham Lewis 1912.*
Coll: Capt. Lionel Guy Baker
Michel (83)

The great Russian writers of the late nineteenth century had an enormous influence on Lewis during his student days in Paris. In *Rude Assignment* he referred to them when he wrote: 'Paris for me is partly the creation of these books. I now realise that if I had not had Tchekov in my pocket I should not have enjoyed my Dubonnet at the 'Lilas' so much or the beautiful dusty trees and beyond them the Bal Bullier. It was really as a character in Tolstoy – I remember now – that I visited a *bal musette*. And the hero of the first novel I wrote reminded a very perceptive critic of Stavrogin.'[1]

Lewis was certainly aware of contemporary Russian art, for example, Fry's Second Post-Impressionist Exhibition of 1912 included a Russian section. However, the theme of the Madonna and Child in this drawing is inspired by the traditional Russian icon.

[1] W.Lewis, *Rude Assignment*, 1950, p.147

Victoria and Albert Museum (E.3762–1919)

17

18

19

19

Sketch for an Abstract Composition

c.1912
Black chalk
$13\frac{1}{2} \times 19\frac{1}{2}$ (34·5 × 49·5)
Unsigned
Coll: Helen Saunders
Michel (85)

A preparatory sketch showing the beginnings of colour notes and giving an indication of Lewis's working methods. Although Lewis did not meet Bomberg until the end of 1912,[1] his sketch shows an awareness of Bomberg's development towards abstraction and particularly his *Vision of Ezekiel* of 1912.

[1] see Cork, pp.82–3

Private Collection

20

22

Sunset among the Michelangelos

c.1912
Pen and ink, gouache
$12\frac{3}{4} \times 18\frac{7}{8}$ (32·5 × 48)
Signed: *Wyndham Lewis*.
Coll: Capt. Lionel Guy Baker
Michel (88)

Lewis felt, as did the Futurists, that European art was obsessed by the great painters of the Italian High Renaissance and Michelangelo in particular. The study of Michelangelo was part of every English art student's training. In his *Review of Contemporary Art*, Lewis wrote: 'Michelangelo is probably the worst spook in Europe, and haunts English art without respite.'[1] In his review of the London Group exhibition in 1915, Lewis stated: 'Michelangelo is my Bête-Noir.'[2] Perhaps Lewis's satirical reference to Michelangelo here is an attempt to purge himself of this 'spook' by transforming the massive Michelangelesque nudes into his own personal vision of the human form.

[1] *Blast No.2*, reprinted in *Wyndham Lewis on Art*, eds W.Michel and C.J.Fox, 1969, p.69
[2] Reprinted ibid., p.86

Victoria and Albert Museum (E.3759–1919)

20

Two Women
also called The Starry Sky

1912
Pencil, pen and ink, watercolour, gouache, collage on grey paper
$18\frac{1}{2} \times 24\frac{1}{2}$ (46·5 × 62)
Signed: *Wyndham Lewis. 1912.*
Coll: John Quinn; Richard Wyndham
Michel (86)

A strange and fantastic distortion of form derived from Cubism but taken to further extremes so that the figures seem to be chiselled out of the ground. No hint of background is given. The figures have been cut out and pasted onto grey paper. The John Quinn sale catalogue paradoxically gives the title as *The Starry Sky*.

The Arts Council of Great Britain

21

Two Mechanics

c.1912
Pen and ink, watercolour
$22 \times 13\frac{1}{4}$ (56 × 33·5)
Unsigned
Coll: Andrew Forge
Michel (114)

Probably the drawing exhibited in 1913 with the more appropriate title *Two Workmen*.[1] It is particularly close stylistically to *Two Women* (cat.20), although the hesitant use of line makes it appear a more experimental and unresolved work in comparison. The pose of the two figures anticipates Epstein's *Studies for Rock Drill* of the following year (see cat.32).

[1] Post-Impressionist and Futurist Exhibition, Doré Galleries, October 1913 (188)

The Trustees of the Tate Gallery (T.108)

21

22

23

The Audition

c.1912–13
Pen and ink, watercolour
$11\frac{1}{4} \times 8\frac{5}{8}$ (28·5 × 22)
Signed: *Wyndham Lewis*
Coll: Capt. Lionel Guy Baker
Michel (119)

The majestic figure of the actor in suitably
theatrical pose is made comic by the
inclusion of the two small figures listening
intently. The tubular, mechanical rendering
of the forms anticipates the robot-like
figures of 1917, for example, *Two
Missionaries* (see cat.47).

Victoria and Albert Museum (E.3782–1919)

24

At the Seaside

1913
Pen and ink, watercolour
$18\frac{3}{4} \times 12\frac{3}{8}$ (47·5 × 31·5)
Signed: *Wyndham Lewis 1913.*
Coll: Capt. Lionel Guy Baker
Michel (123)

A curious mixture of styles showing Lewis's
eagerness to experiment. The literary
content is clearly important to the artist but,
for the spectator, is obscure. Richard Cork
quotes Clive Bell's perceptive criticism of
Lewis in Bell's review of the Post-
Impressionist and Futurist Exhibition at the
Doré Galleries of 1913. Bell wrote: 'He is

inclined to modify his forms in the interests
of drama and psychology to the detriment
of pure design. At times his simplifications
and rhythms seem to be determined by a
literary rather than a plastic conception.'[1]

[1] Cork, p.126

Victoria and Albert Museum (E.3763–1919)

25

Cactus

1913
Pen and ink, watercolour, pastel
$13\frac{3}{8} \times 9\frac{1}{4}$ (34 × 23.5)
Signed: *Wyndham Lewis. 1913.*
Coll: Capt. Lionel Guy Baker
Michel (124)

23

24

25

Reproduced in *Dial*, January 1921 as *Summer Musicians*, it is closely related to *The Musicians* (see cat.27). It also shows an awareness of Matisse and can be compared with, for example, Matisse's *La Musique* of 1911.

Victoria and Albert Museum (E.3768–1919)

26

Composition

1913
Pencil, pen and ink, watercolour
13½ × 10½ (34 × 26·5)
Signed: *Wyndham Lewis. 1913.*
Michel (125)

Although signed and dated 1913, Cork dates the work to 1913–14.[1] It was exhibited at the Redfern Gallery[2] as a later drawing of the 'Timon' series and is particularly close to *Timon of Athens* (Michel 154, not in exhibition).

Lewis produced an outstanding group of watercolours and drawings, only one of which survives, originally intended for a special edition of Shakespeare's *Timon of Athens*.[3] When the series was first exhibited at Fry's Second Post-Impressionist Exhibition held at the Grafton Galleries in October 1912, they attracted considerable attention.[4] They were eventually published in 1913 in the form of a portfolio containing twenty drawings on sixteen sheets of paper. (See illus. pp.61,62) Ezra Pound, whose own copy of the portfolio is included in the exhibition, wrote: 'If you ask me what his "Timon" means, I can reply by asking you what the old play means. For me his designs are a creation on the same *motif*. That *motif* is the fury of intelligence baffled and shut in by circumjacent stupidity. It is an emotional *motif*. Mr. Lewis's painting is nearly always emotional.'[5]

Works like these put Lewis at the forefront of the modern movement. The heavy black structures of *Composition* relate to another abstract composition with the satirical title *Portrait of an Englishwoman* (Wadsworth Atheneum, Hartford, not in exhibition), reproduced in the Russian magazine *The Archer* in 1915 and which may have had a considerable influence on Malevich and the development of Suprematism.[6]

[1] Cork, p.126
[2] Redfern Gallery, *Wyndham Lewis*, 1949 (10)
[3] see Michel (91–109, 154, 174)
[4] see Cork, p.43
[5] Ezra Pound, 'Vorticism', *Fortnightly Review*, 1st September 1914
[6] see Cork, p.128

The Trustees of the Tate Gallery (5886)

27

The Musicians

c.1913
Pen and ink, wash
12 × 9 (30·5 × 22·9)
Unsigned
Michel (144)

The strongly faceted forms of the two figures outlined against a blank background link the drawing to *Two Women* of the previous year (see cat.20).

Private Collection

27

26

28

Portrait of a Woman

c.1913
Pen and ink, watercolour
19 × 12 (48·5 × 30·5)
Unsigned
Coll: Helen Saunders
Michel (148)

The sitter is probably Helen Saunders
(1885–1963) a fellow Vorticist who sat for
two other drawings from this period (see
Michel 147,149). Contemporary
photographs show Miss Saunders to be of
slender build and clearly Lewis was not
attempting an accurate likeness. The
simplification of form and the flowing line
are strongly reminiscent of Matisse.

Private Collection

In 1913 Roger Fry persuaded Lewis to join
his Omega Workshop, and Lewis exhibited
at its opening in July. The permanent rift
between Fry and Lewis in October, after the
Ideal Home rumpus (see p.17), is well
known. In *Rude Assignment* (p.123) Lewis
wrote scathingly of the period: 'By the time
I joined the Omega Workshop – Roger
Fry's abortive venture – my position was
that of an extremist, I suppose: much
further to the left that is, than any of the
others. That was in 1913. I worked there

28

29

with several of my friends and future associates. Frederick Etchells was, I think, the most technologically minded of us: but with no preliminary workshop training it was idle to suppose that half a dozen artists could cope with all – or indeed any – of the problems of waxing, lacquering, polishing, painting and varnishing of furniture – chairs, tables, cabinets and so forth – or the hand-painting of textiles which the plan involved. Naturally the chairs we sold stuck to the seats of people's trousers; when they took up an Omega candlestick they could not put it down again, they held it in an involuntary vice-like grip. It was glued to them and they to it.'

29

Three Figures: Study for a Screen
1913
Pencil and wash
$20\frac{1}{8} \times 15$ (51 × 38·3)
Unsigned
Coll: Roger Fry
Not listed in Michel

One of the few identifiable works by Lewis from the Omega Workshop and very close to *Design for a folding screen* (see cat.30). An uncharacteristically delicate, even insipid drawing, showing Lewis making a conscious effort to fit in with the Bloomsbury style of the other Omega designers.[1]

[1] see Cork, p.87

Courtauld Institute of Art (Fry Collection)

30

Design for a folding screen
1913
Pencil and watercolour
$20 \times 15\frac{1}{4}$ (51 × 38·5)
Unsigned
Coll: Margery Fry
Michel (131)

A more finished design than cat.29, it was shown at the opening of the Omega Workshop in July 1913. The group of circus entertainers, a clown and acrobats, make especial reference to Picasso's pre-Cubist work.

The only other identifiable work by Lewis produced at the Omega is a design for a rug, 1913 (Victoria and Albert Museum, reproduced Cork, p.91).

Victoria and Albert Museum (E.735–1955)

30

The period from October 1913 to the early months of 1914 is the most significant for the development of Vorticism. Lewis had achieved some notoriety as an extremist artist at the forefront of the avant-garde. He exhibited a considerable body of work, most of which is lost, and in March 1914 the financial backing provided by Kate Lechmere enabled him to found the Rebel Art Centre. The movement's gathering momentum culminated in the publication of *Blast No.1* on 2 July 1914. Lewis had been moving steadily towards abstraction for some time, and *Abstract Design* of 1912 (Michel 29, not in exhibition) is considered to be the earliest non-representational composition in British twentieth-century art.

31

The Enemy of the Stars
1913
Pen and ink, wash
$17\frac{1}{4} \times 7\frac{7}{8}$ (44 × 20)
Signed: *Wyndham Lewis 1913*
Coll: John Quinn; Richard Wyndham
Michel (143)

The Enemy of the Stars was the title of a play Lewis published in *Blast No.1*. The drawing was first exhibited in the London

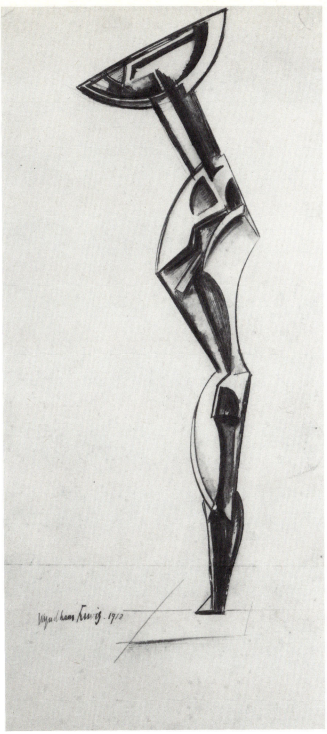

51

Group exhibition of 1914 as *Enemy of the Stars (drawing for sculpture)*. Kate Lechmere considered that Lewis executed the drawing in direct emulation of Epstein's *Female Figure in Flenite*.[1] In turn, the drawing seems close to, and may have influenced, Gaudier-Brzeska's cut brass sculpture *Ornement torpille* of 1914.[2]

[1] see Cork, p.120
[2] repr. Cork, p.444

Private Collection

32

Arghol

1914
Pen and ink, watercolour
13 × 8 (33 × 20·5)
Signed: *W Lewis 1914*
Coll: John Quinn; Richard Wyndham; David Cleghorn Thomson
Michel (159)

Arghol is the hero of Lewis's play *The Enemy of the Stars* (see cat.31). A confident and powerful drawing in which Lewis consolidates his view of man as a robot-like machine. Lewis was undoubtedly inspired by Epstein's studies of 1913 for the *Rock Drill*.[1]

[1] see Cork, pp.468–9

Private Collection

33

Planners (Happy Day)

c.1913
Pencil, pen and ink, gouache
12¼ × 15 (31 × 38)
Signed: *Wyndham Lewis*.
Coll: John Quinn; Richard Wyndham
Michel (145)

In a letter to Charles Handley-Read of 2 September 1949, Lewis wrote: 'I would draw your attention to the fact that "The Planners" is a *title* merely found for this drawing for the purposes of exhibition – by Nan Kivell, I think. The way those things were done – are done, by whoever uses this method of expression – is that a mental-emotive (by this is meant subjective intellection, like magic or religion) impulse is let loose upon a lot of blocks and lines of various dimensions, and encouraged to push them around and to arrange them as it will. It is of course not an accidental, isolated, mood: but it is recurrent groups of emotions and coagulations of thinking, as it were, that is involved.'[1] Although this was

written in 1949, it recalls Kandinsky's famous words about his *Improvisation No.30 (Cannons)* of 1913: 'The designation *Cannons* selected by me *for my own use,* is not to be conceived as indicating the "contents" of the picture. These contents are indeed what the spectator *lives,* or *feels* while under the effect of the *form and colour combinations* of the picture.'[2]

The looser, floating structures of *Planners* seems closer to Kandinsky's work than Lewis's other non-representational compositions of this date. Kandinsky exhibited major paintings in London during the years 1909–13 and must have had considerable influence on the English avant-garde.[3]

[1] *Letters*, p.504
[2] Kandinsky's words were published in A.J.Eddy, *Cubists and Post-Impressionism,* Chicago, 1914, pp.125–6
[3] see Cork, p.216

The Trustees of the Tate Gallery (T.106)

34

Vorticist Design

c.1914
Pen and ink, pencil, watercolour
$9\frac{1}{4} \times 7\frac{1}{4}$ (23·5 × 18·5)
Signed: *Wyndham Lewis.*
Coll: H.T.Tucker
Michel (158)

It is difficult not to read into this design the image of a defiant standing figure with head thrown back. The head-dress recalls the female figure wearing a mantilla in *Spanish Dance* of 1914 (Michel 172).

Private Collection

35

Combat No.2

c.1914
Pen and ink, chalk
$10\frac{7}{8} \times 13\frac{7}{8}$ (27·5 × 35)
Signed: *Wyndham Lewis.*
Coll: Capt. Lionel Guy Baker
Michel (161)

A theme which recalls *The Wild Body* stories and Lewis's description of 'phases of a combat or courtship in the insect-world' (see cat.12). The subject was probably inspired by the threat of approaching war. However, John Rothenstein wrote that Lewis was 'always on a war footing; he believed others were likewise disposed ... War played, I think, a considerable part in

32

33

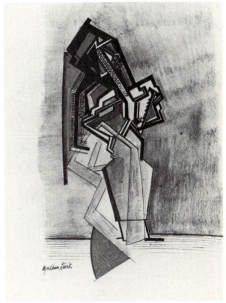

34

35

his imaginative life: he occasionally used military terms to describe his own operations, offensive or defensive, and he alluded more than once to his belonging by birth "to a military caste".[1]

[1] J.Rothenstein, *Brave Day, Hideous Night*, 1966, p.42

Victoria and Albert Museum (E.3760–1919)

36

Combat No.3

1914
Pen and ink, chalk
$10\frac{3}{4} \times 15$ (27·5 × 38)
Signed: *W Lewis 1914*.
Coll: Capt. Lionel Guy Baker
Michel (162)

Lewis adds an uncharacteristic note of pathos by introducing the seated figure with clasped hands. The composition may be a satirical reference to Gauguin's *Vision after the Sermon*.[1]

[1] Kindly suggested to me by Chris Mullen

Victoria and Albert Museum (E.3765–1919)

36

37

37

Ezra Pound (1885–1972)

1914
Pencil and wash
$11\frac{1}{2} \times 10\frac{3}{8}$ (29 × 26·5)
Signed: *W.L. of Ezra Pound. 1914*
Coll: Agnes Bedford
Michel (349)

Ezra Pound, the American poet and critic, met Lewis in 1910.[1] He coined the term 'Vorticism' and became one of the chief publicists of the movement and also an ardent promoter of Lewis's works. He persuaded John Quinn to buy a number of Lewis's paintings and drawings and while Lewis was in the army, Pound acted as his agent in London. It was through Pound that Lewis met T.S.Eliot and James Joyce. They saw less of each other after 1921 when Pound left London, but their friendship lasted until Lewis's death. For other portraits of Pound, see cat.61,68,143,144, 145.

Michel dates the drawing to the year 1919 because of its similarity to the drawing *Ezra Pound* of 1919 (Michel 345). Both drawings harden the sitter's features into an aggressive mask, and both may relate to Lewis's oil portrait of Pound of 1919 (lost, see Michel P26).

[1] see Cork, p.22

Private Collection

The following two works cannot be included in this exhibition because of their fragile state. However, in view of their central importance, photographs and catalogue entries are provided.

38

Workshop

1914–15
Oil on canvas
30 × 24 (76·5 × 61)
Unsigned
Coll: John Quinn
Michel (P19)

Exhibited at the second London Group exhibition and the Vorticist Exhibition of 1915, Lewis seems to have deliberately avoided anything in *Workshop* which might have appeared aesthetically appealing.

Colours are harsh and repellent and the ragged lines in the bottom right area of the canvas give the impression that the picture is unfinished. A clue to the meaning of the title is found in Lewis's novel *Tarr*, written during the winter of 1914–15. The central character, Tarr, refutes Anastasya's declaration that 'all the world's a stage' by declaring that 'it was an actor that said that. I say it's all an atelier – "all the world's a workshop," I should say.'[1] Also, in the first manifesto of *Blast No.1*, England is described as an 'industrial island machine, pyramidal workshop.'[2]

[1] W.Lewis, *Tarr*
[2] see Cork, pp.341–2

Tate Gallery (T.1931–not in exhibition)

39

The Crowd
also called The Revolution

1914–15
Oil on canvas
78 × 60 (198 × 152·5)
Unsigned
Coll: Capt. Lionel Guy Baker; Dr Barnett Stross
Michel (P17)

38

39

First exhibited at the second London Group exhibition in March 1915, it can be compared with Russolo's *The Revolt* which Lewis would have seen in the 1912 Futurist Exhibition at the Sackville Gallery. The diminutive red figures also appear to show the influence of Bomberg's *Mud Bath* of 1912–13. However, a much closer idea of the literary content of the picture can be gleaned from Lewis's story 'The Crowd Master 1914, London, July' published in *Blast No.2* which describes the behaviour of the London crowds in the few weeks before the outbreak of the First World War. It begins: 'THE CROWD. Men drift in thrilling masses past the Admiralty, cold night tide. Their throng creeps round corners, breaks faintly here and there up against a railing barring from possible sights. Local ebullience and thickening: some madman disturbing their depths with baffling and recondite noise.'[1] Lewis connected the crowd with death – 'The Crowd is an immense anaesthetic towards death. Duty flings the selfish will into this relaxed vortex. A fine dust of extinction, a grain or two for each man, is scattered in any crowd like these black London war-crowds. Their pace is so mournful. Wars begin with this huge indefinite Interment in the cities.'[2]

However, the presence of the French tricolour in the bottom left corner of the painting and the two figures brandishing red flags in the middle and upper part of the picture suggest that this is not a London war crowd, but a French socialist one. Lewis was a frequent visitor to Paris in the early years of the twentieth century and a supporter of the Action Française, the proto-Fascist monarchists. The year 1908, in particular, saw months of political unrest centred around the Latin Quarter of Paris. In his unpublished article, '*The Crowd*: Wyndham Lewis and Gustave Le Bon', Chris Mullen makes a convincing comparison between Lewis's painting and Le Bon's *The Crowd. A Study of the Popular Mind* (see cat.3). Le Bon tried to establish certain distinctions between the behaviour of the individual and that of the crowd and also between the behaviour of a Latin and an Anglo-Saxon crowd. He wrote: 'Crowds are everywhere distinguished by feminine characteristics, but Latin crowds are the most feminine of all.'[3] He wrote of the Latin race: 'they have a feminine fickleness which was already noted by the Great Conqueror [Caesar] as a Gallic infirmity.'[4] In contrast, the Anglo-Saxon crowd was more stolid and wary because each member did not subordinate his individuality to the mental unity of the crowd. The small red robot-like figures that merge into each other are consistent with Le Bon's loss of the individual identity in the mass of the crowd. The individual 'is no longer himself... but has become an automaton who has ceased to be guided by his will.'[5] The larger figures in the bottom left corner stand apart from the violence like military leaders at a battle-field. Their heads are capped with black domes, the seat of the intellect. They are the leaders or 'Crowd Masters'. The words 'ENCLO' could perhaps stand for 'Enclosure' or the French equivalent 'Enclos'.

[1] *Blast No.2*, p.94
[2] ibid., p.94
[3] Gustave Le Bon, *The Crowd. A Study of the Popular Mind*, 1913 edition, T.Fisher Unwin, p.44
[4] Le Bon, *The Psychology of Socialism*, 1899, p.129
[5] Le Bon, *The Crowd*, pp.34–5

Tate Gallery (T.689–not in exhibition)

Designs for a Vorticist Sketchbook 1914–15

40

Composition III
1914–15
Pencil and watercolour
$11 \times 10\frac{1}{4}$ (27·9 × 26)
Unsigned
Michel (180)

One of a series of twenty outstanding designs which, like all Lewis's best Vorticist work, has an architectural monumentality. The delicate use of wash strengthens the impression of a row of windows, but for Lewis this was coincidental. In *Blast No.2* he wrote: 'A Vorticist, lately, painted a picture in which a crowd of squarish shapes, at once suggesting windows, occurred. A sympathiser with the movement asked him, horror struck, "Are not those windows?" "Why not?" the Vorticist replied. "A window is for you actually A WINDOW: for me it is a space, bounded by a square or oblong frame, by four bands or four lines, merely." [1]

[1] *Blast No.2*, p.44, see Cork, p.340

Anthony d'Offay

41 see colour plate II

New York

1914
Pen and ink, watercolour
$12\frac{1}{4} \times 10\frac{1}{4}$ (31 × 26)
Signed: *W.L.* and on mount: *Wyndham Lewis . 1914.*
Coll: Edward Wadsworth
Michel (177)

The most fully worked drawing of the series. Lewis did not visit New York until the late 1920s, and the title of the work may have been invented by Wadsworth. However, Lewis must have seen and been influenced by the photography of Alvin Langdon Coburn and, in particular, Coburn's famous *House of a Thousand Windows, New York* of 1912 which Lewis would have seen at Coburn's Exhibition *Camera Pictures* held at the Goupil Gallery in October 1913.[1]

[1] see Cork, pp.495–6

Private Collection

42

Composition V

1914–15
Pencil
$12\frac{1}{4} \times 10\frac{1}{4}$ (31·1 × 26)
Unsigned
Michel (186)

Perhaps the closest drawing in the sketchbook to the architectural designs of the Futurist Antonio Sant' Elia. It has a strong vertical emphasis and Richard Cork makes a convincing comparison with it and Sant' Elia's sketch *Architectural Dynamism* of c.1913–14.[1]

[1] Cork, p.338

Anthony d'Offay

43

Composition in Blue

1915
Ink, crayon and watercolour
$18\frac{1}{2} \times 12$ (47 × 30·5)
Signed: *W.Lewis 1915.*
Coll: Helen Saunders; Helen Peppin
Michel (196)

Lewis had a tendency to overwork his abstract designs so that drawings like *Composition* (cat.26) become heavy and oppressive. However, the freedom of the design of *Composition in Blue* gives it a sense of space and depth which makes it a particularly compelling work.

Anthony d'Offay

40

42

44

Vorticist Composition

1915
Pen and ink, black chalk and gouache
$15\frac{1}{4} \times 8\frac{1}{8}$ (39 × 20·5)
Signed: *Wyndham Lewis . 1915*
Coll: Helen Saunders
Michel (211)

According to Helen Saunders, the drawing was once framed by Lewis in silver foil which must have produced a startling effect.[1] It shows the characteristically diagonal stress to the architectural forms which gives the composition an unstable quality as if the whole structure is toppling over.

[1] Cork, p.334

The Trustees of the Tate Gallery (T.625)

43

44

45

45

The Psychologist
also called The Great Vegetarian

1917
Pen and ink, watercolour
$6\frac{1}{2} \times 5\frac{1}{8}$ (16·5 × 13)
Signed: *Wyndham Lewis 11/7. 1917* and *III C.S.*
Coll: Capt. Lionel Guy Baker
Michel (257)

Similar to the 1909 heads such as *Anthony* (cat.2) and *Architect with Green Tie* (Michel 12), the distortions of the face still owe a debt to German Expressionism. It can be compared with, for example, Emil Nolde's *Head* of 1912–13 (Scottish National Gallery of Modern Art). Nolde had parallel interests in Oceanic and African art and also masks and the theme of dance. Lewis had written a sensitive and favourable review of an exhibition of German woodcuts in *Blast No.1*.[1]

The ruled paper and the small piece of perforated paper glued down to the left of the head indicate that the work is a an experimental sketch.

[1] *Blast No.1*, p.136, reprinted in *Wyndham Lewis on Art*, eds Walter Michel and Cy Fox, 1969, pp.39–40

Victoria and Albert Museum (E.3773–1919)

46

Pastoral Toilet

1917
Pen and ink, watercolour
$6\frac{7}{8} \times 8\frac{1}{2}$ (17·5 × 21·5)
Signed: *VII C.S. W.L. 1917.* and *Wyndham Lewis 14/7/17 VIIC.S.*
Coll: Capt. Lionel Guy Baker
Michel (256)

Similar to the rather whimsical drawings of musicians of 1913 (see cat.nos.24, 26).

Victoria and Albert Museum (E.3772–1919)

47

Two Missionaries
also called First Meeting – Feelings Mixed

c.1917
Black crayon
$12 \times 13\frac{3}{4}$ (30·5 × 35)
Signed: *Wyndham Lewis.*
Coll: Capt. Lionel Guy Baker
Michel (259)

As in *The Wild Body* stories, Lewis shows the same telling observation of the comic aspect of human behaviour. The figures appear to be a visual manifestation of Lewis's vision of humans as puppets or automatons. Stylistically, the work is closest to the combat drawings of 1914.

Victoria and Albert Museum (E.3771–1919)

46

47

In March of 1916, Lewis enlisted and began a period of training with the Royal Artillery in England before being sent to the Western Front as a gunner and bombardier. It was Captain Guy Baker who persuaded Lewis to apply to become an Official War Artist. In December of 1917, Lewis was seconded to the Canadian Corps Headquarters at Vimy Ridge and was commissioned to paint a picture for the Canadian War Memorials Fund (*A Canadian Gun Pit* – Michel P22, not in exhibition). In the following year, the Imperial War Museum commissioned *A Battery Shelled* (not in exhibition, see illus. above) completed in 1919.

Lewis's work as a war artist enabled him to put on his first one-man show, *Guns*, at the Goupil Gallery in February 1919. His experiences on the Western Front are vividly recounted in *Blasting and Bombardiering*. Like many young artists who witnessed the devastation caused by trench warfare, the hellish landscape had a gruesome fascination for him – 'Those grinning skeletons in field-grey, the skull still protected by the metal helmet: those festoons of mud-caked wire, those miniature mountain-ranges of saffron earth, and trees like gibbets – these were the properties only of those titanic casts of dying and shell-shocked actors, who charged this stage with a romantic electricity.' (*B & B*, p.131).

48

Walking Wounded
1918
Pen and ink, crayon, watercolour
10 × 14 (25·4 × 35·6)
Signed: *P.Wyndham Lewis / 1918.*
Coll: A.G.Tansley
Michel (322)

One of the most powerful of the series of war drawings. The high viewpoint and metallic gleam of the bodies make the figures resemble struggling insects. Lewis was fascinated by insect life and owned a heavily annotated copy of John Lubbock's *Ants, Bees and Wasps*.

The Trustees of the Imperial War Museum

49

Battery Position in a Wood
1918
Pen and ink, crayon, watercolour
12½ × 18½ (32 × 47)
Signed: *P.Wyndham Lewis 1918.*
Michel (267)

Again, as in many of the war drawings, Lewis uses a high viewpoint which gives a sense of detachment and may indirectly show the influence of Japanese art. Lewis admired the same detachment in Uccello's *Rout of San Romano*. In the introduction to the *Guns* exhibition catalogue, he wrote of the picture: 'It does not borrow from the *fact* of War any emotion, any disturbing or dislocating violence, terror or compassion – any of the psychology that is proper to the events of War. A Japanese warrior with his ferocious mask, is more frigid than the classic masks of Mantegna's despairing women. Uccello's battle-piece is a perfectly placid pageantry.'[1]

[1] W.Lewis, Introduction to catalogue for exhibition *Guns by Wyndham Lewis*, Goupil Gallery, 1919, reprinted in Michel, p.434

The Trustees of the Imperial War Museum

50

Battery Pulling In (II)
1918
Pencil, pen and ink, watercolour
14 × 20 (35·5 × 51)
Signed: *Wyndham Lewis 1918*
Coll: Charles Rutherston
Michel (269)

Charles Rutherston noted down the following description taken from the exhibition catalogue to *Guns by Wyndham Lewis*, Goupil Gallery, 1919 (52): 'When a Heavy or Siege Battery pulls in to a new position the site for the guns has already been allotted, and in the case of a gun using a platform, the gun emplacement has to be dug out and the platform placed in position. The stores are brought up in lorries, unloaded and placed in a convenient position beside the gun to which they belong.'

City of Manchester Art Galleries (1925. 488)

51

Drag Ropes
c.1918
Pencil, pen and ink, watercolour
14 × 16¼ (35·5 × 41·5)
Signed: *Wyndham Lewis.*
Coll: Charles Rutherston
Michel (273)

Lewis does not attempt to record a specific event or location, but has isolated the two groups of men who are pulling one of the large guns into position (see cat.50).

City of Manchester Art Galleries (1925. 487)

52

Great War Drawing No.2
c.1918
Pen and ink, watercolour
15¼ × 21⅝ (38·5 × 55)
Unsigned
Michel (276)

73

48

74

49

50

52

The drawing does not appear to have been
exhibited in the *Guns* exhibition, but it may
be a study for a painting, *Practice Barrage*,
which was exhibited (no.38 – Michel P23,
whereabouts unknown). Lewis's description
of the painting in the catalogue corresponds
closely to the drawing. He wrote: 'In this
painting officers and signallers are seen in
trenches or dug-outs within sight of the
enemy, observing the fire of their own
Batteries, barrages and so on. It is their duty
to range their Batteries on different
objectives, give details of the result of fire,
accounts of hostile shelling, movements,
etc.'

Southampton Art Gallery

53

The Howitzer
also called Laying

c.1918
Pen and ink, watercolour
14 × 20 (35·5 × 51)
Unsigned
Coll: John Quinn; Richard Wyndham
Michel (283)

The drawing was described in the Quinn
sale catalogue (1927) as 'A vigorous
rendering of a gun crew: erect, virile figures,
wearing leather jerkins, and the No.4 laying
the gun. At the left are sandbags, and the
drapings of a camouflage. Before a deep-

51

75

gold sky.' Under the *Guns* exhibition catalogue entry for his drawing *The No.2* (Michel 295), Lewis had written: 'Each of the gun crew has his number, each having a particular function. The No.4 for instance is the man who lays the gun and nothing else.'

The Arts Council of Great Britain

54

The Menin Road

c.1918
Pen and ink, watercolour
$12 \times 18\frac{1}{2}$ (30·5 × 47)
Signed: *W Lewis.*
Coll: John Quinn; Richard Wyndham
Michel (288)

Formerly called *Great War Drawing No.1*, Michel quotes a letter from Quinn to Lewis dated 16 June 1919 (Dept. of Rare Books, Cornell University) in which Quinn describes *The Menin Road* as 'a battery with one big gun near the upper right; a shovel in the centre; a man over at right; four figures in centre, two men in lower left looking at the landscape at upper left. Lower left corner shows a box with the butts of nine shells.' As in *Great War Drawing No.2* (cat.52) Lewis has chosen a more panoramic composition which shows the line of guns, camouflaged by netting, receding into the distance.

Southampton Art Gallery

55

The Rum Ration

c.1918
Crayon and watercolour
$13\frac{1}{4} \times 9\frac{1}{2}$ (33·5 × 24)
Signed: *W.L.*
Coll: Philip Granville
Michel (308)

Lewis wrote in the *Guns* exhibition catalogue: 'At the nightly serving out of the rum ration in a Battery, an officer has always to be present. The sergeant is here seen with the rum bottle, and men coming in through the door of the dug-out with their dixies.'

According to a typed sheet glued to the backboard, Philip Granville visited Lewis at his studio in Notting Hill Gate on 20 July 1956 with the purpose of asking Lewis to sign the watercolour. Lewis, by then blind, initialled the drawing in the presence of his wife.

Sheffield City Art Galleries

53

54

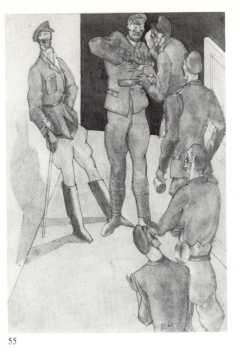

55

56

56

'D' Sub-section Relief

c.1918
Pen and ink
14 × 20 (35·5 × 51)
Signed: *Wyndham Lewis*
Coll: Olivia Shakespear; Dorothy Pound
Michel (274)

Michel refers to a letter of 3 September 1919 to Quinn in which Lewis describes a drawing *D-Subsection Relief going up* as one of the best in the *Guns* exhibition.[1] As in *Walking Wounded* (cat.48), the high viewpoint together with the arbitrary way that figures are cut off by the picture edge, gives a sense of detachment.

[1] John Quinn Memorial Collection, New York Public Library

Private Collection

During the early post-war years, Lewis went into semi-retirement and began an intense period of work. He wrote later: 'The War, of course, had robbed me of four years, at the moment when, almost overnight, I had achieved the necessary notoriety to establish myself in London as a painter. It also caught me before I was quite through with my training. And although in the "post-war" I was not starting from nothing, I had to some extent to begin all over again.'
(*B & B*, p.123)

Lewis's reputation as a draughtsman rests on the drawings done from life during the years 1919–21. The incisive control of line present in the Vorticist work is taken to a more sophisticated level in both the drawings and paintings, such as *Praxitella* (see cat.79). The prolific achievement of these few years must be regarded as a peak in Lewis's career.

57

L'Ingénue

1919
Pencil, red chalk and wash
20 × 13⅞ (51 × 35)
Signed: *Wyndham Lewis. 1919.*
Coll. Charles Rutherston
Michel (334)

The title *L'Ingénue* (the innocent) is not a reflection of the character of the sitter, but was more likely a title inspired by the appearance of the finished drawing. A similar loose tunic appears again in *Reading* (cat.60) which is probably of the same sitter.

City of Manchester Art Galleries (1925. 495)

58

The Lascar

1919
Pen and ink, wash
12 × 10½ (30·5 × 26·5)
Signed: *W.L. 1919.*
Michel (336)

The same model appears in a small group of drawings of the same date (see Michel 353, 341, 342, 355). The exotic title 'Lascar' – an East-Indian sailor – was probably suggested to Lewis after the drawing's completion.

Whitworth Art Gallery, University of Manchester

58

57

59

Nude

1919
Black crayon, watercolour and gouache
11 × 15 (28 × 38)
Signed: *Wyndham Lewis 1919.*
Coll: Charles Rutherston
Michel (340)

A rich and heavy use of colour which is closest to the drawing *Red Nude* (Michel 351). The same model was probably used in two other drawings (see Michel 339 and 384). Lewis drew a number of stooping and crouching female nudes at this date, concentrating on the way the forms were concertinaed together.[1]

[1] see Michel (357, 365 and 366)

City of Manchester Art Galleries (1925. 575)

60

Reading

c.1919
Pencil, watercolour and red chalk
20 × 14 (51 × 35.5)
Unsigned
Coll: Charles Rutherston
Michel (350)

A soft and delicate use of shading in which Lewis's hand and incisive line plays a less prominent part. A model with a sleeping cat appears again in a drawing of the same date (Michel 361).

City of Manchester Art Galleries (1925. 489)

61

Ezra Pound

c.1919
Pencil and watercolour
14 × 15 (35.5 × 38)
Unsigned
Coll: Miss M.S.Davies
Michel (347)

A pose reminiscent of the 1938 oil portrait of Pound (see cat.143). The use of graduated tones of wash to create form and volume is close to the nude studies of the same date, for example, *The Lascar* (see cat.58). Lewis often accentuated outline by adding a line of colour around a particular form, like the head, as here. It can be compared with *Man with a Pipe* (see cat.66 – and also Michel 392 and 378).

The National Museum of Wales

59

62

Girl Looking Down

1919
Black crayon
11½ × 14½ (29 × 37)
Signed: *W Lewis 1919.*
Michel (329)

An outstanding drawing in the series, showing a particularly controlled use of line. The sitter is a Mary Webb.

The Vint Trust

63

Girl Seated

1920
Pencil and blue wash
14⅜ × 10 (36 × 25.5)
Signed: *Wyndham Lewis. 1920.*
Coll: Charles Rutherston
Michel (392)

The sitter is possibly Madge Pulsford who was a friend of Frederic Etchells and of Helen Saunders. The drawing was exhibited in the Tate Gallery exhibition of 1956.[1] Miss Pulsford wrote in a letter to the Tate Gallery in 1956: 'As to No.68 in the present exhibition I am not so certain though the pose is of me. I can't remember the frock but can't even remember what sort of frocks I wore in 1920. When at the exhibition with Miss Helen Saunders and knowing there was a drawing of me there I took No.68 to be it as I passed through the doorway and only later on realised it was not the named No.62. Miss Saunders was doubtful but agreed the pose was of me.

'Wyndham Lewis wasn't drawing a commissioned portrait. He had some idea of a Triptych of types in his mind and was using me for one and may have been drawing to his own purpose more than usual.'

In addition to the second drawing referred to (Michel 373), there are three other studies of the same sitter (see cat.64, 72 and Michel 418).

[1] Tate Gallery, *Wyndham Lewis and Vorticism*, 1956 (68)

City of Manchester Art Galleries (1925. 512)

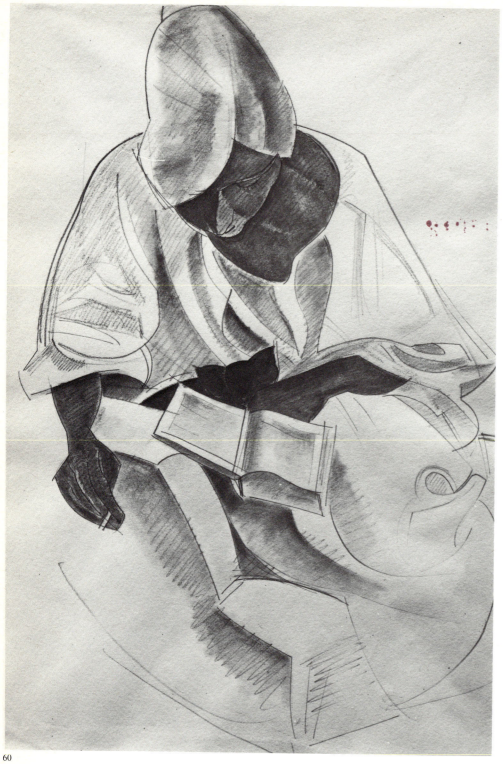

60

61

62

63

64

65

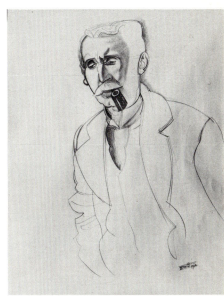

66

64

Girl Seated

1920
Pencil
$15\frac{3}{4} \times 20\frac{3}{8}$ (39·5 × 51·5)
Signed: *Wyndham Lewis 1920*.
Coll: Charles Rutherston
Michel (394)

The sitter is Madge Pulsford. The drawing is very similar to another (Michel 373) where the sitter wears the same dress.

City of Manchester Art Galleries (1925. 511)

65

Lady in a Windsor Chair

1920
Black crayon
22×15 (56 × 38)
Signed: *W Lewis 1920*
Coll: Charles Rutherston
Michel (400)

In a number of drawings of this date, Lewis left the eyes blank, producing the impression of a lifeless mask, and, together with the low viewpoint, the effect is hieratic. The deliberate omission of the eyeballs in the drawing recalls Lewis's remarks about the treatment of the eyes in his own self-portrait of 1921 (see cat.78). They have no highlights in order not to give 'the wrong kind of life' to the head. Lewis was interested in the external appearance of the sitter and not in an inner psyche.

City of Manchester Art Galleries (1925. 212)

66

Man with a Pipe

1920
Pencil and red wash
$20 \times 14\frac{3}{4}$ (51 × 37·5)
Signed: *W Lewis 1920*.
Coll: Charles Rutherston
Michel (405)

The sitter was a London cabby who was a favourite model and who appears in a number of other drawings of the same period (see Michel 385, 386, 471).

City of Manchester Art Galleries (1925. 231)

67

68

69

67

Nude

1920
Black crayon and red wash
15 × 19½ (38 × 49·5)
Signed: *W Lewis 1920.*
Coll: Charles Rutherston
Michel (406)

An unusually pale and delicate use of wash which foreshadows Lewis's frequent use of pastel washes of colour on his portrait drawings of the late 1920s and 1930s.

City of Manchester Art Galleries (1925. 496)

68

Poet Seated : Ezra Pound

c.1921
Black crayon
14¾ × 19 (37·5 × 48·5)
Signed: *Wyndham Lewis.*
Coll: Charles Rutherston
Michel (409)

Lewis would endeavour to draw his sitters once they had relaxed into a characteristic pose. This portrait drawing of Pound is reminiscent of Lewis's words: 'Ezra now lay flung back in a typical posture of aggressive ease.'[1] The mask-like depiction of the face in many of the drawings of this date is taken a step further here and the poet's head resembles an African or Oceanic carving. It resembles two other drawings of Pound, both dated 1921 (Michel 473 and Private Collection, not listed in Michel). The same chair appears in many works of the period (see cat.69, 73, 79 and Michel 390, 393, 496).

[1] *B & B*, p.283

City of Manchester Art Galleries (1925. 507)

69

Miss 'E'

c.1920
Black crayon
14¾ × 22 (37·5 × 56)
Unsigned
Coll: Charles Rutherston
Michel (389)

The sitter is the daughter of Edwin Evans (see cat.92). She appears in a similar drawing (Michel 390).

City of Manchester Art Galleries (1925. 508)

70

71

70

Portrait of a Girl Standing

c.1920
Black crayon on buff paper
16½ × 10 (42 × 26·5)
Unsigned
Coll: Charles Rutherston
Michel (410)

Lewis's interest in hats extends in portraits to details of costume. Buttons, pleats and patterned cloth all contribute to the strength of the design. It can be compared with, for example, the pencil drawing of *Edith Sitwell* (see cat.96).

City of Manchester Art Galleries (1925. 210)

71

Profile of a Girl's Head

1920
Black crayon
14 × 10 (35·5 × 25·5)
Signed: *W Lewis 1920.*
Coll: Charles Rutherston
Michel (416)

A stark and powerful treatment of a profile head – volume and solidity are just as convincing in the areas which are not shaded. The sitter wears the same low-necked loose garment as in *L'Ingénue* (cat.57) although the two drawings do not appear to be of the same person.

City of Manchester Art Galleries (1925. 209)

72

Drawing of Madge Pulsford

1920
Pencil and watercolour
15 × 11 (38 × 28)
Signed: *WL 1920.* and *DRAWING OF MADGE PULSFORD. / 1920. / WYNDHAM LEWIS.*
Coll: Miss Madge Pulsford
Michel (417)

The distinctive facial features of the sitter make it surprising that Miss Pulsford thought that *Girl Seated* (cat.63) was also a portrait of herself. It is very close to a second drawing at the Tate Gallery (Michel 418). This includes an interior with some colour notes and appears to be a study for a painting.

The Trustees of the Tate Gallery (T.193)

73

Study for Painting (Seated Lady)

1920
Pencil, wash and gouache
$14\frac{3}{4} \times 10\frac{3}{4}$ (37·5 × 27·5)
Signed: *Wyndham Lewis 1920*.
Coll: Charles Rutherston
Michel (433)

Probably a study for *Praxitella* (cat.79). As in *Poet Seated: Ezra Pound* (cat.68) the head resembles a primitive mask, and in Lewis's autobiography, *Rude Assignment*, it was reproduced with the rather unlikely and facetious title, *Cave Woman in a Chair*.

City of Manchester Art Galleries (1925. 505)

74

Edward Wadsworth (1889–1949)

c.1920
Black crayon and wash
$15\frac{1}{4} \times 11$ (38·5 × 28)
Signed: *Wyndham Lewis*.
Michel (436)

Wadsworth's early career was closely associated with Lewis and their friendship lasted until the 1920s. Born in Yorkshire, Wadsworth studied engineering at Munich in 1906. He later studied at the Bradford School of Art where he gained a scholarship to the Slade School and was a Slade student from 1908–12. He exhibited in the Second Post-Impressionist Exhibition and later joined the Omega Workshop where he met Lewis. He left with Lewis in October 1913 and joined the Rebel Art Centre. He exhibited at the Post-Impressionist and Futurist Exhibition and at the Allied Artists' Association in 1913, 1914 and 1916. He was included in the 'Cubist Room' section in the Camden Town Exhibition of 1913 and was a foundation member of the London Group. He signed the manifesto in *Blast No.1* where he published translations of extracts from Kandinsky's *Über das Geistige in der Kunst* under the heading 'Inner Necessity'. He contributed to the 1915 Vorticist Exhibition and his work was reproduced in *Blast No.2*. He served in the Royal Naval Volunteer Reserve as Intelligence Officer until invalided out in 1917, and was later employed designing dazzle camouflage for ships. After the war, he exhibited with Lewis's Group X but he changed his style and moved away from Vorticism. In the 1930s he became

74

73

75

associated with Unit One and with the English Surrealists.

Lewis would often begin a drawing and then turn the sheet the other way up, as here, and begin again – see *The Courtesan* (cat.11). For other drawings of Wadsworth, see Michel (435, 437, 438).

Pembroke College, Oxford, Junior Common Room

75

Woman Knitting

1920
Pencil
19½ × 13 (49·5 × 33)
Signed: *W.Lewis. 1920.*
Coll: Charles Rutherston
Michel (440)

City of Manchester Art Galleries (1925. 234)

76

Lady Seated at Table

1921
Pencil
10⅞ × 10½ (27·5 × 26·5)
Signed: *Wyndham Lewis. 1921*
Coll: Charles Rutherston
Michel (467)

One of a group of drawings which relate to *Praxitella* (see cat.79).

City of Manchester Art Galleries (1925. 506)

77

Self-portrait

1920
Pen and wash
7 × 8¾ (18 × 22)
Signed: *Self-portrait. Wyndham Lewis. 1920.*
Coll: Douglas Ainslie
Michel (423)

Lewis produced a large number of self-portraits at this period. He exhibited seven at the Group X exhibition of 1919 and a group of self-portraits the following year have the same hard and dramatic highlighting as here.[1] William Rothenstein remembers meeting Lewis in c.1922 and asking him to sit for a portrait drawing. Lewis replied, 'I am sitting for myself at present – in fact it is a permanent job, and I never sit for anybody else!'[2]

[1] see Michel (426, 429, 430)
[2] William Rothenstein, *Men and Memories, 1900–22,* 1932, p.378

The Vint Trust

76

78 see front cover

Portrait of the Artist as the Painter Raphael

1921
Oil on canvas
30 × 27 (76 × 68·5)
Signed: *Wyndham Lewis*
Coll: Charles Rutherston
Michel (P28)

Charles Rutherston noted that this self-portrait was painted in April 1921, bought in during the Leicester Gallery exhibition,[1] and exhibited there during May without a number, but with a placard on which the above title was typed. Lewis could have been drawing a parallel with Raphael's own self-portrait in the Uffizi or identifying himself with a great classical artist of the Renaissance period.[2] Although Lewis's views on classicism and romanticism are often paradoxical, Lewis considered himself to be a classical artist. He defined classicism in art as, 'a *progress* backward . . . to the great, central, and stable canons of artistic expression, *away from* the atmospheric, impressionistic, molecular – pointilliste, vibratory – plein-air nineteenth century aesthetic.'[3] To achieve this in his own art, Lewis concentrated exclusively on the external appearance of things. The rigid, stable forms of this *Self-portrait* recall Tarr's definition of the two most important conditions of art as deadness and absence of soul – 'Anything living, quick and changing is bad art always . . . Deadness is the first condition of art: the second is absence of

soul, in the human and sentimental sense.'[4] Significantly, Lewis remarked to Michael Ayrton that there are no highlights on the eyeballs of the self-portrait because it would give the wrong kind of life to the head.[5] No doubt glinting eyes would hint at an unstable inner psyche. The strident and startling colour contrasts of *Self-portrait* recall *Workshop* (see cat.38).

[1] Leicester Galleries, *Tyros and Portraits*, 1921
[2] see J.Farrington, 'Wyndham Lewis and a prescient collector,' *Apollo*, Jan. 1980, pp.48–9
[3] W.Lewis, 'Creatures of Habit and Creatures of Change,' *The Calendar of Modern Letters*, April 1926, pp.17–44, cit. in G.D.Bridson, *The Filibuster: A Study of the Political Ideas of Wyndham Lewis*, 1972, p.60
[4] W Lewis, *Tarr* (first publ. 1918, second edn rewritten 1928), Calder and Boyars: Jupiter Books, 1968, pp.279–80
[5] Michel (423), p.337

City of Manchester Art Galleries (1925. 579)

79 see colour plate III

Praxitella

1920–1
Oil on canvas
56 × 40 (142 × 101·5)
Signed: *Wyndham Lewis*
Coll: Edward Wadsworth
Michel (P30)

In a letter to John Quinn of 18 April 1921, Lewis wrote: 'As regards the show, I have at length, in truth, begun painting. "Praxitella", a portrait of myself "as the painter Raphael" (it is not in catalogue; I have just put it in): the Tyros reading Ovid, The Tyro about to breakfast etc.: are more realised that anything I have done. I can't talk about them myself, except to say that as paintings they are in the same category of completion as my drawings: only more so, I think, because a complete painting, being more complex and on a fuller scale, has invariably the advantage over a drawing.'[1]

The sitter is Iris Barry (1895–1970), the writer and film critic. She was born near Birmingham, and educated at Birmingham, Wantage and in Belgium. Ezra Pound discovered her early published poems and persuaded her to try her luck in London. During the First World War she frequented a literary circle which included Pound, Eliot, Lewis, Ford Madox Ford and Arthur Waley. She had a prolonged and unhappy affair with Lewis, living with him from 1918–1921, and had two children by him. She became film critic for *The Spectator* and later the *Daily Mail*. In 1925, with Anthony

77

Asquith, Ivor Montague, Sidney Bernstein, McKnight Kauffer and Edmund Dulac, she co-founded the London Film Society. Miss Barry created the Film Library at the Museum of Modern Art in New York with her second husband, John 'Abbott, and became its first curator.

The same dress with the striped underskirt appears in a number of portrait drawings of this date, probably with the same sitter (see cat.73, 76).[2]

The title of the painting may refer to the Greek sculptor Praxiteles in the same way that *Self-portrait of the Artist as the Painter Raphael* refers to a classical artist of the past (see cat.78). The faceted surface of the head is reminiscent of Picasso's portrait heads of 1909 and the olive-green flesh tones recall German Expressionist portraits.

[1] John Quinn Memorial Collection, New York Public Library – quoted in Michel (P34)
[2] see also Michel (450, 459, 466, 476, 496, 498)

The Leeds City Art Gallery

80

Self-portrait as a Tyro

1920–1
Oil on canvas
$29\frac{7}{8} \times 17\frac{7}{8}$ (75·9 × 45·4)
Unsigned
Coll: Sidney Schiff; Sir Edward Beddington Behrens; Mrs. E.Gluck
Michel (P27)

Tyros first appeared in the *Tyros and Portraits* exhibition held at the Leicester Galleries in April 1921. Lewis described these works as a series of pictures coming under the heading of satire. The garish colour and angular distortion of *Self-portrait as a Tyro* are deliberately repellent. In the catalogue foreword, Lewis wrote: 'These Tyros are not meant to be beautiful, that they are, of course, forbidding and harsh, there will, no doubt, be found people who will make this discovery with an exclamation of reproach. Swift did not develop in his satires the comeliness of Keats, nor did Hogarth aim at grace. But people, especially in this country, where satire is a little foreign, never fail to impeach the artist when he is supposed to be betraying his supreme mistress, Beauty, and running after what must appear the strangest gods.'[1] Lewis described the Tyro as an elemental person. 'These immense novices brandish their appetites in their faces, lay bare their teeth in a valedictory, inviting, or merely substantial laugh.'

The threatening shape of the hat is an important part of the Tyro image. Lewis, himself, had a taste for flamboyant headwear and invariably sported an aggressive example (see cat.77, 78, 112). It is significant that the characters of Lewis's novel are often made more vivid by the description of their headwear.

1 Reprinted in Michel, p.437

Ferens Art Gallery, City of Kingston-upon-Hull

81 see colour plate IV

A Reading of Ovid (Tyros)

1920–1
Oil on canvas
65 × 35 (165 × 89)
Unsigned
Coll: Sir Osbert Sitwell
Michel (P31)

One of the most successful works from the Tyro series. In a letter to John Quinn of 2 May 1921, Lewis wrote: 'The "Tyros Reading Ovid" . . . is one of the paintings I took longest over, is very carefully painted: as a fragment of a large composition it is quite successful as regards colour. The very strong reds of the hands and faces [are] set in the midst of grey-blues and strong blues. It is quite a satisfactory painting: it would make a good Altarpiece.'[1]

Lewis's satirical view of people was of automatons or puppets trying to behave with the dignity and assurance of human beings. In Lewis's collection of short stories, *The Wild Body*, published in book form in 1927, Lewis added a chapter entitled 'The Meaning of the Wild Body' in which he wrote: 'The root of the Comic is to be sought in the sensations resulting from the observations of a *thing* behaving like a person. But from that point of view all men are necessarily comic: for they are all *things*, or physical bodies, behaving as *persons* . . . To bring vividly to our mind what we mean by 'absurd' . . . Suppose you came upon an orchid or a cabbage reading Flaubert's 'Salammbô', or Plutarch's 'Moralia', you would be very much surprised. But if you found a man or a woman reading it, you would *not* be surprised. Now in one sense you ought to be just as much surprised at finding a man occupied in this way . . . There

is the same physical anomaly. It is just as absurd externally, that is what I mean. – The deepest root of the Comic is to be sought in this anomaly.'[2] It is, therefore, comic and ridiculous to see two Tyros perusing the work of a classical author with their blank stares and fixed grins.

1 John Quinn Memorial Collection, New York Public Library, quoted in Michel, p.337
2 W.Lewis, *The Wild Body and other stories*, 1927, pp.247–8

Scottish National Gallery of Modern Art

82

The Broombrush

c.1921
Pen and black ink
19¾ × 15 (50 × 38)
Unsigned
Coll: Agnes Bedford
Michel (449)

The drawing was reproduced in Lewis's magazine *The Tyro No.1*. In the *Daily Express* of 11 April 1921, Lewis was quoted as saying: 'The Tyro is raw and under developed: his vitality is immense, but purposeless, and hence sometimes malignant. His keynote, however, is vacuity; he is an animated, but artificial puppet, a "novice" to real life.'

In a letter to John Quinn of 18 March 1921, he wrote: 'I am doing a book of forty of these Tyro drawings . . . this satire is a challenge to the Arts-for-Arts-sake dilettantism of a great deal of French work to-day (and the Bloomsbury Bell-Grant-Fry section of English).'[1]

1 John Quinn Memorial Collection, New York Public Library, quoted in Michel p.100
With the Maclean Gallery, London.

From the mid-1920s onwards, with the exception of his rôle as art critic, Lewis appears to have become more disinterested in the work of his contemporaries. Whilst continuing to practice portraiture, he experimented with a series of imaginative, semi-abstract drawings inspired by literary, mythological and historical sources. This is not surprising for an artist who devoted the same amount of creative energy to writing as well as painting. Lewis had a catholic taste in literature and his library was extensive.

82

83

83

Abstract Composition

1921
Pen and ink, watercolour
10½ × 9¼ (26·5 × 23·5)
Signed: *Wyndham Lewis 1921*
Michel (442)

During the early years after the war, when Lewis was working on the series of drawings from life, he was also producing abstract work. *Abstract Composition* does not bear much relation to Vorticist art and is more probably a development from the Tyro drawings. Forms are more complex and curvilinear compared with the Vorticist grid-like shapes. The figure to the right is reminiscent of Oskar Schlemmer's doll-like puppets.

Private Collection

84

Abstract Figure Study

1921
Pen and ink, wash
$11\frac{1}{4} \times 6\frac{3}{4}$ (28·5 × 17)
Signed: *Wyndham Lewis. 1921.*
Michel (447)

The complex forms of the figures, resembling totem-poles, are a more obvious development from the Tyro drawings and can be compared with, for example, *Tyro Madonna* (Michel 493).

Harrogate Borough Council Art Gallery

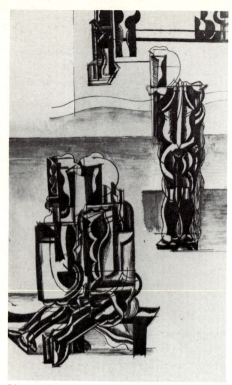

84

85

Abstract Figure Study

1921
Pen and ink, wash
$14\frac{1}{2} \times 12\frac{1}{4}$ (37 × 31)
Signed: *Wyndham Lewis. 1921.*
Coll: Nicholas Guppy
Michel (445)

Comparable with cat.84.

Private Collection

86

Figure Composition

c.1921
Pen and ink, watercolour, pencil
$13\frac{5}{8} \times 17\frac{1}{2}$ (34·5 × 44·5)
Signed: *Wyndham Lewis.*
Michel (456)

The frieze-like grouping of the forms suggests figures on a stage.

Anthony d'Offay

85

87

Contemplator
also called Sensibility

1921
Pen and ink, wash
$12\frac{1}{2} \times 10\frac{1}{4}$ (31 × 26)
Signed: *Wyndham Lewis . 1921.*
Michel (483)

87

A starker and more menacing version of the totem-pole figures of the same year. The small red heart perhaps has a satirical reference. It is closely related to a drawing of the same year reproduced as a frontispiece to Sacheverell Sitwell's *Doctor Donne and Gargantua – First Canto*, published in 1921 (a copy is included in the exhibition, see also Michel 448).

The Vint Trust

88

Edith Sitwell (1887–1964)

1921
Pencil
$17\frac{1}{2} \times 20$ (39 × 28·5)
Signed: *Wyndham Lewis. 1921*
Coll: Sir Osbert Sitwell
Michel (485)

Dame Edith Sitwell, the writer and poet, first met Lewis towards the end of the First World War. He was a frequent visitor to her flat and also to the house of her brothers, Sir Sacheverell and Sir Osbert Sitwell.[1] After the Sitwells were satirised in Lewis's book, *The Apes of God*, their friendship soured. Lewis described Dame Edith as, 'one of my most hoary, tried and reliable enemies. We are two good old enemies,

86

EDITH SITWELL

89

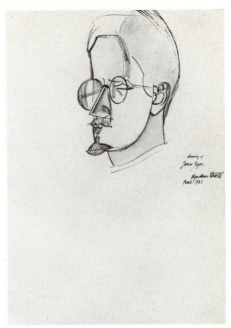

91

Edith and I, *inseparables* in fact. I do not think I should be exaggerating if I described myself as Miss Edith Sitwell's *favourite enemy*.'[2]

An austere and hieratic image which is probably a study for the oil portrait (see cat.113). It also closely relates to two other drawings of the same date (see Michel 486–7). In all three, the sitter wears the sam dress and headdress with a large crucifix around her neck (though only the cord of th crucifix can be seen in this drawing). For other portraits of Edith Sitwell see cat.89, 9

[1] see E.Sitwell, 'Personal Encounters – 3 Hazards of Sitting for My Portrait', *Observer*, 27 November 1960, p.24
[2] *B & B*, p.91

National Portrait Gallery (4464)

89

Edith Sitwell

c.1921
Pencil and watercolour
$15\frac{1}{2} \times 10\frac{1}{4}$ (39·5 × 26)
Unsigned
Michel (488)

A subtle and delicate work in marked contrast to the other more formal drawings of the same sitter.

The Trustees, the Cecil Higgins Art Gallery, Bedford

90

Virginia Woolf (1882–1941)

c.1921
Pencil and wash
15 × 10 (38 × 25·5)
Signed: *Wyndham Lewis.*
Michel (500)

The identity of the sitter is open to question. It was exhibited in 1949 simply as *Woman in Large Hat*.[1] It seems unlikely, after the permanent rift with the Bloomsbury Group in 1913, that Virginia Woolf would have agreed to sit for Lewis. On the few occasions when Mrs Woolf referred to Lewis, it was with some venom. In a letter to Roger Fry of 22 October 1922, she wrote: [Herbert] Read, who has been in the Wyndham Lewis pigsty without wallowing in it, had some amazing stories of the brutes. Lewis now paints in a shed behind a curtain – rites are gone through before you enter . . .'[2]

[1] Redfern Gallery, *Wyndham Lewis*, 1949 (57)
[2] *The Letters of Virginia Woolf, 1912–22*, ed. Nigel Nicolson, 1976, p.573

Victoria and Albert Museum (Circ. 71–1959)

90

91

James Joyce (1882–1941)

1921
Ink and watercolour
$11\frac{3}{16} \times 8\frac{1}{8}$ (28·4 × 20·6)
Signed: *drawing of | James Joyce. | Wyndham Lewis | Paris. 1921*
Not listed in Michel

Lewis drew a number of portrait drawings of Joyce during the years 1920–1.[1] He first met Joyce in Paris in the summer of 1920 when he travelled there with T.S.Eliot.[2] In *Blasting and Bombardiering*, Lewis described a visit to Paris with Charles Rutherston and Frank Dobson: 'My days were spent with Rutherston and Dobson, visiting collections of Chinese art, my nights with James Joyce; an exquisitely balanced arrangement. "The Dante of Dublin", as Mr. Gogarty calls him, cast a dreamy spell over Paris-by-night, and Sung and Ming weighed in, in the day-time, with their more subtle spell.'[3]

[1] see Michel (396, 397, 398, 463)
[2] *B & B*, p.265
[3] ibid., p.235

Sheffield City Art Galleries

92

Edwin Evans (1874–1945)

1922
Oil on canvas
59 × 42½ (150 × 108)
Unsigned
Coll: Edwin Evans
Michel (P35)

Edwin Evans was an influential music critic and champion of modern music. In 1912, he was music critic to the *Pall Mall Gazette*, and from 1919–20 he contributed a series of articles in the *Musical Times* on modern British composers. In 1933, he became music critic to the *Daily Mail*, and in 1938 he was elected president of the International Society for Contemporary Music. He left a valuable library of books on music and scores and sheet music which became the nucleus of the Central Music Library.

On 21 January 1923, his services to the cause of the younger British composers were acknowledged by the presentation to him of his portrait by Lewis, subscribed for by a group of composers. A number of important musicians of the day were present at a dinner held in his honour and at which the portrait was to be presented. They included Arthur Bliss, Stravinsky, de Falla, Ravel and also Augustus John. The portrait commission did not progress smoothly and the painting remained unfinished. Arthur Bliss wrote later: 'The circumstances of the Wyndham Lewis portrait of E.E. were as follows: It was presented to E.E. at a dinner at Pagani's by Eugene Goosens and myself. The portrait was then unfinished, as Wyndham Lewis refused to go on with it unless he was paid more money! As this dribbled in, he added touches to the picture until I think it was practically finished. In the end E.E. said he wanted it as it was and hung it in his house.'[1]

Probably because the portrait remains unfinished, areas of the canvas show that Lewis used the squaring-off technique to enlarge the portrait from a smaller study. Another example where this technique is visible, is the pencil study of *The Sitwell Brothers* (Michel 553). Two drawings of Evans survive (see Michel 529–30).

[1] Letter from Arthur Bliss in Scottish National Gallery of Modern Art files

The Scottish National Gallery of Modern Art

92

93

93

Topsy

1922
Pencil
20¾ × 15½ (52·5 × 39·5)
Signed: *Wyndham Lewis 1922.*
Coll: Charles Rutherston
Michel (555)

An early portrait of the artist's future wife, Gladys Anne Hoskyns (1900–1979). Lewis first met her shortly after the First World War but they did not marry until 1930. She was a devoted wife and frequently modelled for Lewis. The drawing has the same sculptural quality of the life drawings of 1919–21 but, in contrast, Lewis experiments with a thin, feathery technique using delicate pencil shading. For other portraits of the artist's wife see cat.129,133,134,136, 139,140.

City of Manchester Art Galleries (1925. 215)

94 see colour plate v

Red and Black Olympus

1922
Pen and ink, gouache
10 × 17¼ (25·5 × 44)
Signed: *Wyndham Lewis 1922*
Coll: John Hayward; Miss G. Rolleston
Michel (474)

The style of the drawing suggests that it may have been begun at an earlier date. Lewis often post-dated works in the hope that this would make them more saleable. The convoluted mechanical forms recall Duchamp and also Picabia.

Private Collection

95

Archimedes Reconnoitring the Enemy Fleet

1922
Pen and ink, watercolour
13 × 18¾ (33 × 47·5)
Signed: *Wyndham Lewis. 1922*
Michel (519)

Similar to *Abstract Composition*, 1921 (cat.83), where a third or more of the picture space is left blank, the title refers to Archimedes' successful defence against the Romans at the siege of the port of Syracuse. Archimedes devised weapons and engines of war that for three years held the Romans at bay in their siege of the port of Syracuse.

The Vint Trust

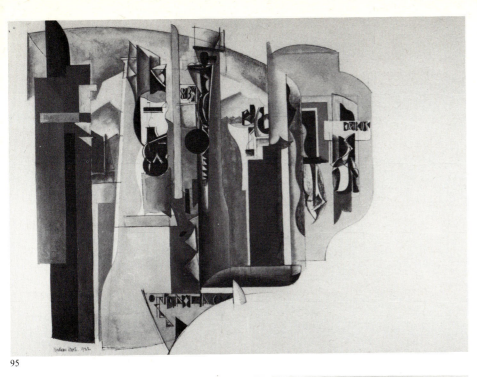

95

96

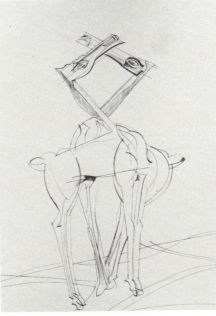

97

96

Edith Sitwell

1923
Pencil and wash
$15\frac{3}{4} \times 11\frac{3}{8}$ (40 × 29)
Signed: *Wyndham Lewis. 1923.*
Coll: Sir Osbert Sitwell
Michel (592)

An example of the delicate and feathery
technique found in many of the pencil
portraits of this date.

National Portrait Gallery (4465)

97

Drawing of Horses

1923
Pen and ink
$18 \times 12\frac{1}{2}$ (45·5 × 31·5)
Signed: *W Lewis 1923*
Coll: Agnes Bedford
Michel (572)

Very similar to a drawing reproduced in *The
Tyro No.2* with the title *Drawing for
Jonathan Swift* (Michel 526). Lewis
particularly admired Swift's satirical writing
and blessed Swift in *Blast No.1* for his
'solemn bleak wisdom of laughter'. Lewis's
own brand of literary satire has often been
compared to Swift.

Private Collection

98

Three Arabs

c.1926
Black ink
$9 \times 4\frac{1}{2}$ (23 × 11)
Unsigned
Coll: Agnes Bedford
Michel (673)

The drawing was intended to illustrate
T.E.Lawrence's book *The Seven Pillars of
Wisdom*. Lewis described his first meeting
with Lawrence in his autobiography,
Blasting and Bombardiering.[1] Lawrence had
asked Lewis to do some drawings to add to
the illustrations for the book in 1925.[2]
Lewis wrote later: 'I did a set of drawings
for his [Lawrence's] book – not so quickly
as I should, and all of a sudden I heard it
had appeared to my great disappointment.'[3]
The Seven Pillars of Wisdom was published
in December 1926.

[1] *B & B*, pp.238–45
[2] see Michel (615)
[3] *B & B*, p.244

Private Collection

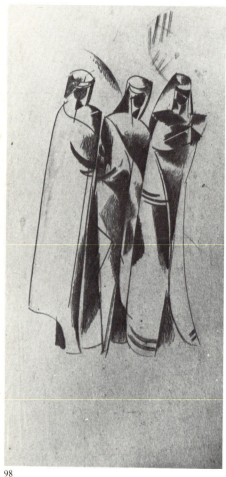

98

99

100

99

Hero's Dream
also called Dawn in Erewhon and The
Dream of Hamilcar

1925
Collage, watercolour, pen and ink
10¼ × 6¾ (26 × 17)
Signed: *W.L.1925*.
Coll: Curtis Moffat; Shearsby
Michel (614)

Hamilcar Barca (d. 229 B.C.) was a
Carthaginian commander in the First Punic
Wars and father of Hannibal. He devoted
his military career to a war of revenge
against Rome. Erewhon is an anagram of
'nowhere' used by Samuel Butler
(1835–1902) in two satirical novels
Erewhon: or Over the Range and *Erewhon
Revisited*.

Private Collection

100

The Sibyl

1926
Pen and ink, watercolour
8¾ × 5½ (22·2 × 14)
Signed: *Wyndham Lewis 1926*.
Michel (624)

The stunted limbs of the sibyl are
characteristic of Lewis's semi-abstract
figures of the late 1920s and can be
compared with, for example, *Figures in the
Air* of 1927 (see cat.105).

Private Collection

96

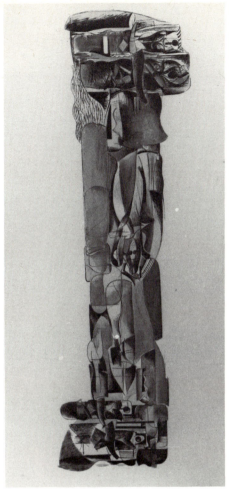

101

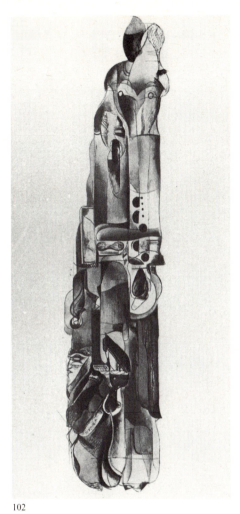

102

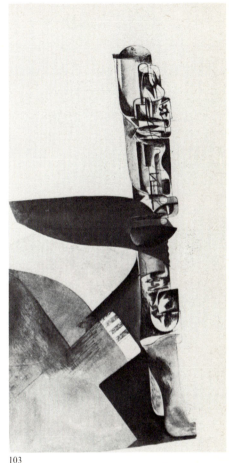

103

101

Abstract Composition

1926
Pen and ink, watercolour, pencil
22 × 10⅜ (56 × 26.5)
Signed: *WL26*
Coll: Mrs Olivia Shakespear
Michel (617)

One of a group of three drawings done for Mrs Shakespear's dining room (see cat.102, 103). Olivia Shakespear, an admirer and patron of Lewis's work, was the mother of Dorothy Shakespear (1886–1973) the Vorticist artist who married Ezra Pound. In a letter to Olivia Shakespear of 1 June, 1925, Lewis wrote: 'I have a scheme which may or may not appeal to you. It is this. Between now and September the first I shall be generally finishing and proof-correcting my various books, but I should like to do

some drawing too with a definite object and I should like to provide three designs for one of your walls. I should aim at finishing one a month, the third to be finished and in place anyway by Sept. the first.'[1] The subject-matter of the drawings clearly held some significance for Lewis. In a letter of 4 June to Mrs Shakespear he wrote: 'I will tell you the idea I had for the group.'[2]

All three drawings anticipate the vertical complex of forms in *Bagdad* (see cat.104).

Lewis's interest in insect life and, in particular, the cross-section diagrams of insects,[3] may have inspired the forms of these three drawings.[4]

[1] Dept. of Rare Books, Cornell University Library
[2] ibid.
[3] Lewis owned a heavily annotated copy of John Lubbock's *Ants, Bees and Wasps*
[4] Richard Humphries kindly pointed out this connection.

Private Collection

102

Abstract Composition

1926
Pen and ink, watercolour, pencil
$22 \times 10\frac{3}{8}$ (56 × 26.5)
Signed: *W.L. 26*
Coll: Mrs Olivia Shakespear
Michel (618)

Private Collection

103

Abstract Composition

1926
Pen and ink, watercolour, pencil
$19\frac{5}{8} \times 9\frac{5}{8}$ (50 × 24.5)
Unsigned
Coll: Mrs Olivia Shakespear
Michel (619)

Private Collection

104

Bagdad

1927
Oil on plywood
72×31 (183 × 79)
Unsigned
Coll: Curtis Moffat
Michel (P38)

The plywood panel is composed of several strips joined together. Lewis is known to have done decorations for one or more cupboards for his studio in Ossington Street during the late 1920s. *Bagdad* is reputed to be one such decoration.[1] The Piranesi-like spiral staircase suspended in space appears to be a development from drawings of the previous year, for example, the group of three *Abstract Compositions* (see cat.101–3). The title may be connected with Lewis's story, 'The Parable of the Caliph's Design'[2] which is set in Baghdad.

[1] see Michel (P42)
[2] W.Lewis, *The Caliph's Design*, The Egoist Ltd, 1919

The Trustees of the Tate Gallery (T.99)

105

Figures in the Air
also called On the Roof

1927
Pencil, pen and ink, watercolour
$11\frac{1}{2} \times 6\frac{1}{2}$ (29.5 × 16.5)
Signed: *WL. 1927.*
Michel (635)

The skewered figures and tilting perspective produce a sinister and disturbing composition. A reclining manikin-like form with stunted limbs occurs frequently in imaginative drawings of the period, for example, *Manhattan* (see cat.106 and Michel 609, 661).

The Vint Trust

106

Manhattan

1927
Pen and ink
$14\frac{1}{2} \times 9\frac{3}{4}$ (37 × 25)
Signed: *Wyndham Lewis 1927.*
Michel (637)

Lewis visited New York for the first time in 1927 for the purpose of selling his work. The grid-like structures are reminiscent of the Vorticist *New York* (cat.41) but otherwise the two drawings have little in common. In a letter of 1 August 1927 from the Hotel Brevoort, Fifth Avenue, Lewis wrote to C.H.Prentice: 'The high buildings are very impressive, especially the later ones "hanging-gardens" style. The earlier ones are like particularly long-necked cathedrals or big English parish churches.'[1] The group of figures surging forward recall the central figure in *Heroic* (see cat.132).

[1] *Letters*, p. 169

The Vint Trust

107

Creation Myth No.2

Collage, pen and ink, watercolour
$13\frac{3}{8} \times 11$ (34 × 28)
Signed: *Wyndham Lewis.*
Coll: Arthur Crossland
Michel (658)

The theme of creation was a recurring one in Lewis's art. In a letter from Paris of c.1903, Lewis wrote: 'I'm installing myself there today, and begin a series of paintings and drawings of the Creation of the World.'[1] Lewis showed a painting entitled *Creation* at the Allied Artists' Association in July 1912. He said that the 'Creation Myth' was a phantasy of the worlds moving round together in a chaotic corner of creation. The idea of 'Creation' is always a beginning of a spontaneous growth.[2]

Creation Myth No.2 was exhibited at the Redfern Gallery in 1949 and dated 1933 in the catalogue.[3] The hard, diagonal structure reminiscent of the Vorticist abstractions, suggests that the work may have been begun at an earlier date.

[1] *Letters*, p.10
[2] see Tate Gallery exhibition catalogue, *Wyndham Lewis and Vorticism*, 1956 (87)
[3] Redfern Gallery, *Wyndham Lewis*, 1949 (86)

The Whitworth Art Gallery, University of Manchester

108

Creation Myth No.3
also called Abstract: harbour

1930
Pen and ink, watercolour
$9\frac{1}{2} \times 11$ (24 × 28)
Signed: *Wyndham Lewis. 1930.*
Michel (676)

A rapidly sketched drawing in which the forms whirl around in a primeval chaos. The title suggests that it is related to *Creation Myth Nos.1 and 2* but, according to the Redfern exhibition catalogue, these were both executed in 1933[1] (see cat.107 and Michel 787).

[1] Redfern Gallery, *Wyndham Lewis*, 1949 (86, 88)

The Vint Trust

104

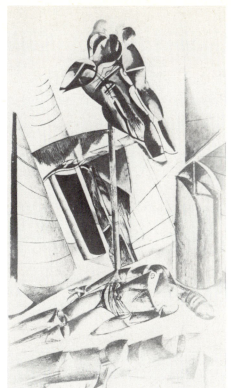

105

107

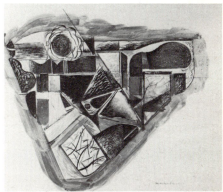

108

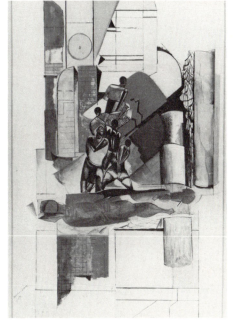

106

109

110

111

109

Portrait of a 'Blue Woman'

1931
Pencil and watercolour
14 × 9½ (35·5 × 25)
Signed: *Wyndham Lewis 1931*
Coll: Dorothy Pound
Michel (719)

In the spring of 1931, Lewis and his wife travelled to North Africa. They visited the Atlas Mountains where the rugged landscape and primitive architecture of the Berber tribesmen inspired both the artist's painting and writing. A series of articles about his travels were published in *Everyman* magazine and later in book form, *Filibusters in Barbary* of 1932. In an article 'The Blue Sultan' published in *The Graphic*, 7 November 1931, Lewis wrote that the 'Islamised Berbers who in 1910 came up out of the Western Sahara and invaded Morocco ... were called "Blue Men" because of their indigo cottonades ... with which their bodies became stained'. The drawing closely relates to one of a full figure, seated cross-legged (Private Collection – not in Michel).

Private Collection

In 1932 Lewis held an exhibition at the Lefevre Galleries entitled Thirty Personalities, a collection of thirty pencil portraits which included a number of celebrated figures of the day. It was followed by a published portfolio entitled *Thirty Personalities and a Self-portrait*. In the catalogue introduction, Lewis stated that, with the exception of two, all the drawings were done during the months of July and August 1932. The slick, insipid quality of many of the drawings together with the defensive tones of Lewis's catalogue introduction, suggest that the venture was a pot-boiling one. Lewis wrote of the drawings: 'Coming from the workshop of an extreme experimentalist, they may at first be regarded rather as a demonstration of traditional draughtsmanship. They are not that. I have always practised side by side the arts of experiment and arts of tradition. To an artist there seems no contradiction in this – it only seems contradictory to the outsider, or the person imperfectly acquainted with the aims of the artist.'

110

Duncan Macdonald (d.1949)

1932
Pencil
15 × 11 (38 × 28)
Signed: *Wyndham Lewis 1932*
Michel (774)

Duncan Macdonald was one of the founding directors of the firm of Alex Reid & Lefevre, art dealers, in 1926. He remained with the firm, except for a few years during the war, until his death.

The Syndics of the Fitzwilliam Museum, Cambridge

111

Miss Rebecca West (b.1892)

1932
Chalk
13 × 10 (33 × 25·5)
Signed: *Wyndham Lewis. 1932*
Michel (786)

Lewis met Rebecca West, the writer, before the First World War. In *Rude Assignment*, he wrote: 'It was at dinner at Mrs Hueffer's (Mrs. Ford Madox Ford) for instance that I first met Rebecca West. She was a dark young maenad then, who burst through the dining-room door (for she was late) like a thunderbolt.'[1]

Rebecca West contributed a short story, 'Indissoluble Matrimony' to *Blast No.1*. She was an admirer of Lewis's writings and wrote a number of perceptive reviews of his books. Lewis considered her to be one of the two or three acutest critics in England.[2]

[1] W.Lewis, *Rude Assignment*, 1950, p.122
[2] ibid., p.202

Dame Rebecca West

112

Self-portrait with Hat

1932
Pen and ink, watercolour
10 × 7½ (27·5 × 21·5)
Signed: *WL 1932*.
Coll: J. Paton Walker
Michel (782)

A defiant and aggressive image which has satirical overtones. It was reproduced in *The Daily Herald* of 30 May 1932 with an article by Lewis, 'What it feels like to be an Enemy'. It is particularly close to a self-portrait of 1931, entitled *Self-caricature* (Michel 725).

National Portrait Gallery (4528)

113

113

Edith Sitwell (1887–1964)

1923–35
Oil on canvas
34 × 44 (86·5 × 112)
Signed: *Wyndham Lewis*
Coll: Sir Edward Beddington-Behrens
Michel (P36)

In a letter of 8 January 1951 to Lady Snow,
Edith Sitwell wrote of Lewis: 'I knew him
well, because I sat to him every day

excepting Sundays, for ten months. It was
impossible to like him, and in the end, his
attitude became so threatening that I ceased
to sit for him, so that the portrait of me by
him in the Tate has no hands, and I figured
as Lady Harriet in his 'The Apes of God'.
(And he figured as Mr. Henry Debringham
in the only novel I have written, 'I Live
Under a Black Sun') . . . When one sat to
him, in his enormous studio, mice emerged
from their holes, and lolled against the

furniture, staring in the most insolent
manner at the sitter. At last, when Tom
Eliot was sitting to him, their behaviour
became intolerable. They climbed on to his
knee, and would sit staring up at his face. So
Lewis bought a large gong which he placed
near the mouse-hole, and, when matters
reached a certain limit, he would strike this
loudly, and the mice would retreat.'[1]
The artist's wife remembers that the head,
the coat and the legs were finished when the

114

115

painting was abandoned. In c.1935, Lewis painted in the forearms and the background and made some alterations to the coat. For portrait drawings of the same sitter, see cat.88, 89, 96.

[1] E.Sitwell, *Selected Letters*, eds John Lehmann and Derek Parker, 1970, p.231

The Trustees of the Tate Gallery (5437)

The mid-1930s produced a series of oil paintings of an often fantastic and dream-like world peopled by pin-headed automatons. This was also an important period for Lewis's imaginative writings and although he never discussed his paintings in relation to his novels, undoubtedly there must be a connection between the two.

114

Abstract

1932
Oil on canvas
$18\frac{1}{4} \times 13\frac{1}{2}$ (46·5 × 34·5)
Signed: *Wyndham Lewis 1932.*
Coll: Arthur Crossland
Michel (P44)

One of the first of a series of oils of the 1930s, showing a simplified treatment of the human form, often with stunted limbs and a blank sphere for the head. According to the Alfred East Art Gallery accession card, the contemplative figure squatting in eerie surroundings depicts the artist in his studio. The deep blue patch at top right is the night sky.

Alfred East Art Gallery, Kettering

115

The Convalescent
also called The Invalid

1933
Oil on canvas
24 × 30 (61 × 76·5)
Signed: *Wyndham Lewis 1933.*
Coll: Fairfax Hall; Sir Colin and Lady Anderson
Michel (P46)

The two figures, given the faces of manikins, are surrounded by a semi-abstract world of slatted forms except for the startling realism of the still-life group of crockery in the foreground. The subject-matter perhaps has an autobiographical reference. Lewis

suffered from frequent and prolonged bouts of illness at this period.

Glynn Vivian Art Gallery and Museum, Swansea

116 see colour plate VI
Inca with Birds

1933
Oil on canvas
27 × 22 (68·5 × 56)
Signed: *Wyndham Lewis 1933*
Coll: Mrs Lynette Roberts
Michel (P49)

The source for the subject-matter is taken from W.H.Prescott, *The History of the Conquest of Peru* first published in 1847. Lewis admired the writings of Prescott and owned a copy of this particular work. Prescott refers to the 'Royal Commentaries' of Garcilasso de la Vega, an Inca and native of Peru who witnessed the Spanish conquest. Garcilasso records the Inca tradition that the Inca ruler wore a headdress decorated with feathers taken from the 'Corequenque' birds. These feathers had black and white bands and had to come from both a male and female bird.

104

Prescott wrote: 'The birds from which these feathers were obtained were found in a desert country among the mountains; and it was death to destroy or to take them, as they were reserved for the exclusive purpose of supplying the royal head-gear. Every succeeding monarch was provided with a new pair of these plumes, and his credulous subjects fondly believed that only two individuals of the species had ever existed to furnish the simple ornament for the diadem of the Incas.'[1]

[1] W.H.Prescott, *The History of the Conquest of Peru*, edition edited by John Foster Kirk, p.12. I am indebted to Richard Humphries for pointing out this source.

The Arts Council of Great Britain

117

One of the Stations of the Dead

1933–7
Oil on canvas
50 × 30½ (127 × 77·5)
Signed: *Wyndham Lewis 1933*
Coll: Naomi Mitchison
Michel (P50)

Although dated 1933, it was not completed until 1937. In *Rude Assignment* Lewis referred to the paintings of this period when he wrote: 'I have varied between realist fantasies and semi-abstraction. The satiric realism of *Beach Babies* and the semi-abstract *Stations of the Dead*.'[1]

The concepts of immortality, heaven and hell, and the underworld held a fascination for Lewis in the latter part of his career in both his writing and painting, for example, *The Immortality of the Soul* and *Negro Heaven* (see cat.123, 153). In his writing this can be paralleled with the descriptions of heaven and hell in the trilogy, *The Human Age*.[2] Water and, in particular, the sea, is present in a large number of Lewis's imaginative paintings, for example, *The Surrender of Barcelona* and *Creation Myth No.3* (see cat.130, 108) and here it appears in the form of a subterranean river.[3]

[1] W.Lewis, *Rude Assignment*, 1950, p.130
[2] W.Lewis, *The Human Age*, 1955
[3] The theme of the sea in Lewis's art is discussed by Sheila Watson in 'Lewis and the sea', *Arts Canada*, November 1967, p.4

Aberdeen Art Gallery and Museums

117

118

Red Scene

1933
Oil on canvas
$27\frac{7}{8} \times 36$ (71 × 91·5)
Signed: *Wyndham Lewis 1933*
Michel (P52)

The predominantly red-brown subterranean colours and pin-head figures link *Red Scene* to the sinister and surreal series of canvasses of the mid-1930s, such as *Group of Suppliants* and *One of the Stations of the Dead* (see cat.119, 117).

The Trustees of the Tate Gallery (4313)

119

Group of Suppliants

1933
Oil on canvas
30 × 24 (76·5 × 61)
Signed: *Wyndham Lewis 1933*
Coll: W.A.Evill
Michel (P48)

Group of Suppliants and similar paintings of the same date may have been inspired by Dante's *Inferno*, to which Lewis makes specific reference in the chapters describing Hell in the trilogy, *The Human Age*. An eerie atmosphere is created by the characteristically sharp highlighting.

Private Collection

120

Two Beach Babies

1933
Oil on canvas
20 × 24 (51 × 61)
Signed: *Wyndham Lewis 1933*
Michel (P53)

Lewis described this kind of composition as 'satiric realism' (see cat.117). Handley-Read wrote of the painting: 'The pert expression, set to catch the camera-man, is emphasised by the pose which is the satirical epitome of coquettishness at the seaside.'[1] The figures are more like puppets or automatons than human beings. This impression is reinforced by the repetition of pose and facial expression and the simplification of limbs. For Lewis ' "men" are undoubtedly, to a greater or lesser extent, machines … Men are sometimes so palpably machines, their machination is so transparent, that they are *comic*, as we say.'[2]

[1] Charles Handley-Read, *Wyndham Lewis*, 1951, p.55
[2] W.Lewis, *Men without Art*, 1934, p.116

Rugby Borough Council

118

120

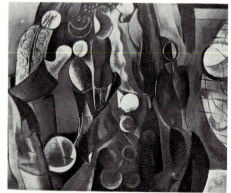

121

121

Creation Myth

c.1933–6
Oil on canvas
$19\frac{1}{2} \times 23\frac{1}{4}$ (49·5 × 59)
Unsigned
Coll: Professor S.Russ
Michel (P54)

The only oil painting in the *Creation Myth* series. The vibrant colour scheme recalls

Lewis's words in a letter to Charles Handley-Read of 2 September 1949 in which he discusses the paintings of this period. He wrote: '*The literary imagination is invited to compose – in a highly selective but far more complex, world of forms – usually dominated by one colour – say saffron, or blue.*'[1]

[1] *Letters*, p.505

New College, Oxford, Junior Common Room

106

119

122

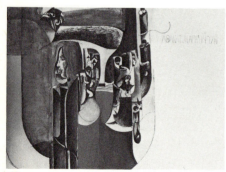

123

124

122

Cubist Museum

c.1933–6
Oil on canvas
20 × 30 (51 × 76)
Unsigned
Coll: David Cleghorn Thompson; Mrs Gabrielle Keiller
Michel (P58)

Spectators closely resemble some of the museum objects and perhaps Lewis is gently poking fun at the group staring earnestly at a small sculptural form, very like an egg. By this date, Lewis was against extreme forms of abstraction. In *The Demon of Progress in the Arts* he wrote: 'Beyond a certain well-defined line – in the arts as in everything else – beyond that limit there is *nothing*. Nothing, zero, is what logically you reach past a line, of some kind, laid down by nature, everywhere.'[1] For Lewis Cubism lacked energy and vitality compared with Vorticism and perhaps he considered that it was destined to be preserved only in museums as a curiosity, divorced from life.

[1] W.Lewis, *The Demon of Progress in the Arts*, 1954, p.32

With David W.Hughes, London

123

The Immortality of the Soul

c.1933
Pen and ink, pencil, watercolour and gouache
9¾ × 13⅞ (24·8 × 35·2)
Unsigned
Inscribed: ΑΘΑΝΑΤΟΝΑΡΑ'ΗΨΥΧΗ
Coll: R. Q. Borthwich
Not in Michel

A similar Greek inscription appears in *Athanaton* (Michel 626) and *Creation Myth No.1* dated 1933 (Michel 787). The latter is the closest to this drawing, with the same floating pin-head figures and a glimpse of a calm blue sea. The inscription can be translated as 'Immortal therefore the soul'.

With the Fine Art Society Ltd, London

124

Boats in Port
also called A Spanish Port

1933
Pencil and gouache
7¾ × 9¾ (19·5 × 25)
Signed: *Wyndham Lewis . 1933.*
Michel (788)

The Vint Trust

125

Naomi Mitchison (b.1897)
also called The Tragic Muse

c.1931
Pencil
18 × 14 (45·5 × 35·5)
Signed: *Wyndham Lewis*
Michel (952)

Naomi Mitchison, the writer, met Lewis in the early 1930s, after she had reviewed *The Apes of God* for *Time and Tide* magazine. Their friendship lasted for the next twenty-five years until Lewis's death. During that time, Lewis drew portraits of most of Naomi Mitchison's family and illustrated her book *Beyond this Limit*, published in 1935.

In the most recent volume of her autobiography, Naomi Mitchison said of Lewis: 'I spent a lot of time and energy trying to persuade him that his quarrels were imaginary, that people didn't really hate him or try to suppress him. We used to argue about all this while he did a whole series of drawings of me. This was in the full Enemy period, the spring and late autumn of 1931. In most of these drawings I am wearing a very formal rose brocade dress which I had bought secondhand in Sarajevo. It had a very low neckline and loose silk-lined sleeves cut away in an odd scallop at the shoulder. He was never tired of the shape of that rather stiff dress, held together at the waist with a big golden brooch; but sometimes in the drawings my hair is close to my head in coils over the ears, and sometimes it is in long corn-coloured plaits. I chose for myself one of the most stylised versions, in which he used me in my dress to suggest something else; he called it *The Tragic Muse*, and it is one of the finest of his drawings.

'Those drawings were all done in the Percy Street studio, where, in the period of the myth, he talked and talked, trying I think to find out if I was or wasn't part of the establishment.'[1]

For other portraits of the sitter, see cat.126, 137.

[1] Naomi Mitchison, *You May Well Ask*, 1979, p.146

Private Collection

126

Naomi Mitchison

1933
Pencil and wash
11 × 9 (28 × 23)
Signed: *Wyndham Lewis 1933*
Michel (792)

The Vint Trust

127

Sir Stafford Cripps (1889–1952)

c.1934
Pen and ink, wash
12½ × 9¼ (32 × 23·5)
Signed: *Wyndham Lewis.*
Coll: ? Arthur Crossland
Michel (842)

The drawing of Sir Stafford Cripps, the politician, was reproduced in *The London Mercury*, October 1934, p.530, opposite a pen drawing of Sir Oswald Mosley (Michel 845), with the caption 'Two Dictators'. Lewis produced a number of pen and ink portrait sketches during the 1930s resulting in a hardening of line and form, for example, *Julian Symons* (see cat.146).

The Trustees, the Cecil Higgins Art Gallery, Bedford

128

Dog Asleep (Tut)

1935
Pencil
7¾ × 12 (19·7 × 30·5)
Signed: *Wyndham Lewis / 1935.*
Not in Michel

Tut was a pet Sealyham dog belonging to the Lewises. Lewis made a number of small, sensitive sketches of the dog during the early 1930s.[1] Tut travelled with the Lewis's to Canada, where he died in 1944, much to Mrs Lewis's distress. In a letter to Felix Giovanelli of 28 January 1944, Lewis wrote of the dog: 'Like the spirit of a simpler and saner time, this fragment of primitive life confided his destiny to her [Froanna], and went through all the black days beside us. She feels she has been wanting in some care – for why should this growth in his side, almost as big as his head, have gone undetected? – Such are the reflections that beset her. Whereas I am just another human being – by no means a well of primitive joie-de-vivre: so not much comfort!'[2]

[1] see Michel 730, 742, 744–5, 768, 780, 794
[2] *Letters*, p.376

Graham Peacock

125

126

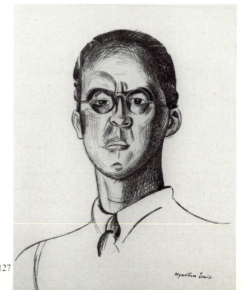

127

128

129

129

Lady on a Sofa – Froanna

c.1936
Black crayon
14 × 21½ (35·6 × 54·6)
Signed: *Wyndham Lewis*
Not in Michel

The sitter is the artist's wife. The sofa appears in three other drawings of the same year (see Michel 861, 874, 880).

Portsmouth City Museum and Art Gallery

130

The Surrender of Barcelona

1934–7
Oil on canvas
33 × 23½ (84 × 59·5)
Unsigned
Michel (P61)

In *Rude Assignment*, Lewis wrote: 'In the *Surrender of Barcelona* I set out to paint a Fourteenth Century scene as I should do it could I be transported there, without too great a change in the time adjustment involved. So that is a little outside the natural-non-natural categories dominating controversy today.'[1] In 1937 Lewis published *The Revenge for Love*, a novel set in the Spanish Civil War, but he denied any connection between this picture and the book.

It seems likely that, as in *Inca with Birds* (cat.116), the writings of W.H.Prescott provide a source for the subject-matter.

Prescott's *History of the Reign of Ferdinand and Isabella* first published in 1837, describes the siege of Barcelona in 1472 by John II of Aragon, which ended in the surrender of the city. The victorious king entered the city at the head of a triumphal procession on 22 December 1472.[2] Lewis's frieze of soldiers in the foreground undoubtedly refers to Velasquez' *Surrender of Breda*, a war picture that Lewis admired. In *Blast No.2*, he referred to it when he wrote: 'Velasquez painted the formality of a great treaty in a canvas full of soldiers.'[3]

[1] W.Lewis, *Rude Assignment*, 1950, p.130
[2] Richard Humphries kindly pointed out this source.
[3] *Blast No.2*, p.26

The Trustees of the Tate Gallery (5768)

131

Landscape with Northmen

c.1936–7
Oil on canvas
26½ × 19½ (67·5 × 49·5)
Signed: *Wyndham Lewis*
Coll: John MacLeod
Michel (P66)

Lewis was fascinated by the warrior explorers of past civilizations and their various forms of battle-dress. This theme occurs in several paintings, for example, *The Armada* (Michel P70) and *Newfoundland* (Michel P67). Lewis also exhibited a painting entitled *Christopher Columbus* (lost) at the London Group Exhibition in March 1914.

The sea is invariably present in Lewis's imaginative compositions, and although *Landscape with Northmen* appears at first to be a landscape of undulating hills, the Viking ship's prow indicates that the figures stand on a shore.

Penelope Allen

132

Heroic

1937
Pen and ink, wash
8¾ × 9¼ (22 × 23·5)
Signed: *Wyndham Lewis 1937*.
Michel (888)

Anthony d'Offay

133 see colour plate VII

Froanna – Portrait of the Artist's Wife

1937
Oil on canvas
30 × 25 (76 × 63·5)
Signed: *Wyndham Lewis.1937*
Michel (P71)

The nickname 'Froanna' was a corruption of 'Frau Anna' which was how a German woman friend in London had addressed Mrs Lewis.[1]

Lewis had Froanna pose in his red dressing-gown which appeared again, this time worn by its owner, in *The Tank in the Clinic* (Miehel P77). Lewis had the ability, in his best portraits, to give even the drabbest clothing a dignity and presence of its own.

131

John Rothenstein singled out for praise the treatment of the lounge suit in Lewis's *Portrait of T.S.Eliot* (cat.147).[2] For other portraits of Froanna, see cat.93, 129, 134, 136, 139, 140.

[1] see *Letters*, p.273
[2] Sir John Rothenstein, *Modern English Painters: Lewis to Moore*, 1956, p.39

Glasgow Art Gallery and Museum

134

Red Portrait

1937
Oil on canvas
36 × 24 (91·5 × 61)
Signed: *Wyndham Lewis 1937.*
Coll: Mrs Eva Handley-Read
Michel (P76)

The sharp highlighting of the blank face, together with the stiff pose, gives the portrait an eerie, lifeless atmosphere. Lewis favoured this dramatically sharp highlighting in a number of pictures of the period, for example *Cubist Museum* (cat.122) and *Group of Suppliants* (cat.119). The sitter is the artist's wife.

W.D. & H.O.Wills

135

Abstract: Ballet Scene

1938
Pen and ink, wash
7 × 9 (18 × 23)
Signed: *Wyndham Lewis 1938.*
Coll: Arthur Crossland
Michel (896)

Reminiscent of the strongly shaded manikin figures of 1925, for example *The Dancers* and *Dancing Couple* (see Michel 610–11).

Bradford Art Galleries and Museums

136

The Full Table

1938
Coloured chalks, wash
14½ × 12¾ (36 × 32.5)
Signed: *Wyndham Lewis 1938*
Michel (903)

A portrait of the artist's wife. The same curved ashtray appears in the oil portrait of Naomi Mitchison of the following year (see cat.137).

Chris and Oriole Mullen

137

Naomi Mitchison (b.1897)

1838
Oil on canvas
40 × 30 (101·5 × 76)
Signed: *Wyndham Lewis*
Michel (P96)

In her autobiography, Naomi Mitchison writes of Lewis: 'He did one big portrait of me in oils, in 1938, where I sit stylised and frowning with a notebook. I was writing 'The Blood of the Martyrs.' I am frowning because I wanted to go on writing the book and had in fact said that I wouldn't sit for him unless I could go on with it; but he couldn't bear me to move, even move one hand, except in the break – ten minutes in the hour. He put a crucifix behind me in the picture somewhat as a tease, while in front as in several of his studio pictures, is the curved ashtray which was always on the table. I didn't really want that crucifix but now I think he was perhaps right; he knew a bit more about me than I knew myself.'[1]

[1] N.Mitchison, *You May Well Ask*, 1979, p.144

Private Collection

132

134

135

136

137

138

Day Dream of the Nubian

1938
Oil on canvas
30 × 40 (76 × 101.5)
Signed: *Wyndham Lewis 1938*
Michel (P78)

Naomi Mitchison posed for the figure
in the picture and, in her most recent
autobiography, describes the painting as of
a 'resting Ethiopian, a beautiful ebony
woman lying on a cushion with one hand
out above the blue stream in front of her
across a corner of the picture. "What is she
doing?" I asked. "Picking a dream out of
the river." "Oh, do put it in!" So he paints
in the shape of a dream and the background
of the picture has a Greek temple front
cutting into a strong pattern of white: this
too for me.'[1]

Naomi Mitchison saw much of Lewis at this
date and remembers discussing with him the
relative importance of African and Greek
civilisations, hence the inclusion of the
Greek temple.

[1] N.Mitchison, *You May Well Ask*, 1979, p.145

Private Collection

138

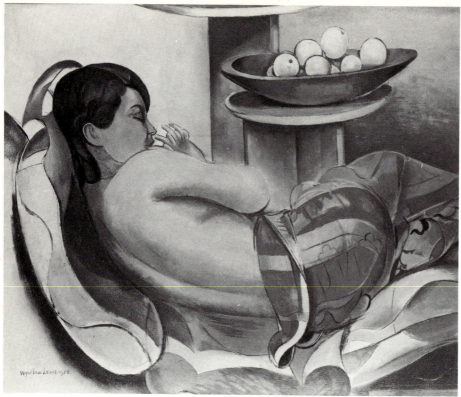

139

141

139

Mexican Shawl

1938
Oil on canvas
25 × 30 (63·5 × 76)
Signed : *Wyndham Lewis 1938*
Coll : Arthur Crossland
Michel (P84)

Lewis's only surviving nude study in oil.
The bowl of oranges has a Cézannesque
precision and acts as a kind òf focal point in
the same way as does the still-life group in
the foreground of *The Convalescent* (see
cat.115). The Art Deco two-tiered wooden
table appears in a number of other portraits
(see cat.143 and Michel P127, P123, P124).
The model is the artist's wife.

The City of Bristol Museum and Art Gallery

140

142

140

Pensive Woman

c.1938
Oil on canvas
23½ × 17½ (59·5 × 44·5)
Signed: *Wyndham Lewis*
Michel (P85)

An intimate and brooding portrait. The sitter is the artist's wife.

Carlisle Museum and Art Gallery

141

Stephen Spender (b. 1909)

1938
Oil on canvas
39½ × 23½ (100·5 × 59·5)
Signed: *Wyndham Lewis 1938*
Michel (P86)

Lewis met Spender, the poet and critic, through Auden while Auden was still a student at Oxford. Lewis wrote: 'Spender, who combines great practical ability with great liberal charm, showed me a lot of jolly poems, mostly about Auden – he said modestly, a much better poet than himself.'[1]

Lewis usually had his sitters pose in the chair seen in this portrait, which appears in numerous others,[2] and as here, Lewis often included in the background details of the studio clutter.

[1] *B & B*, p.250
[2] see cat.147 and Michel (P63, P65, P79, P82, P83, P98)

City Museum and Art Gallery, Stoke-on-Trent

142

Study for Portrait of Stephen Spender

1938
Pencil
19 × 12 (48·5 × 30·5)
Signed: *Wyndham Lewis. 1938. (of Stephen Spender).*
Michel (923)

A sketch for the oil portrait of 1938 (see cat.141). The drawing shows the sitter to be more formally dressed than in the finished oil, but it lacks the force and conviction of the final portrait.

The Vint Trust

143

Ezra Pound

1939
Oil on canvas
30 × 40 (76 × 102)
Unsigned
Michel (P99)

Lewis wrote in his first autobiography: 'In 1938 when I was painting Ezra (the picture is now in the Tate) he swaggered in, coat-tails flying, a malacca cane out of the 'nineties aslant beneath his arm, the lion's head from the Scandinavian North-West thrown back. There was no conversation. He flung himself at full length into my best chair for that pose, closed his eyes and was motionless, and did not move for two hours by the clock. Ezra was not haggard, he looked quite well, but he was exhausted.

'"Go to it Wyndham!" he gruffled without opening his eyes, as soon as his mane of as yet entirely ungrizzled hair had adjusted itself to the cushioned chair-top. A reference to my portrait of Mr Eliot, painted some months earlier, produced the remark that now I had a "better subject to work from". A mild and not unpleasing example of gasconade. But that was how I always found Ezra, full of bombast, kindness, but *always* in appearance the Westerner in excelsis. On the tips of his toes with aggressive vitality, till he dropped, or as good as.'[1]

For other portraits of Pound, see cat.37,61,68, 144,145.

[1] *B & B*, p.286. Lewis gives the date as 1938, but one of the studies is signed and dated 1939 (see cat.145).

The Trustees of the Tate Gallery (5042)

144

Head of Ezra Pound

1938
Black crayon
13 × 10 (33 × 25·5)
Signed: *Wyndham Lewis. 1938.*
Michel (919)

Both this drawing and cat.145 are studies for the 1939 oil portrait of Pound.

The Vint Trust

145

Head of Ezra Pound

1939
Black crayon
14 × 10 (35·5 × 25·5)
Signed: *Wyndham Lewis 1939.*
Michel (938)

City Museum and Art Gallery, Stoke-on-Trent

146

Julian Symons (b.1912)

1938
Pen and ink
13 × 10 (33 × 25·5)
Signed: *Wyndham Lewis. 1938.*
Michel (925)

Julian Symons, the writer, first met Lewis in 1932. He later became editor of the poetry magazine *Twentieth-Century Verse*, which published an issue devoted to Lewis in 1937. Julian Symons saw Lewis most frequently during the years 1937–9, and in 1938 Lewis made three portrait studies of him for an oil portrait begun in 1939 but not completed until 1949.[1] In his article 'Meeting Wyndham Lewis', Mr Symons wrote: 'He made three direct pen drawings of me in less than two hours.'[2]

[1] see Michel (P127, 926, 926A)
[2] *The London Magazine*, October 1956, p.50

Julian Symons

147 see colour plate VIII

T.S.Eliot (1888–1965)

1938
Oil on canvas
52 × 33½ (132 × 85)
Signed: *Wyndham Lewis*
Michel (P80)

Lewis first met Eliot through Pound, in January 1915, a few months before the publication of *Blast No.2* in July 1915, to which Eliot contributed 'Preludes and Rhapsody on a Windy Night'. Lewis remembers Eliot as a 'sleek, tall, attractive transatlantic apparition – with a sort of Gioconda smile.'[1] Eliot contributed to *The Tyro* magazine and Lewis to *The Criterion*. Their friendship lasted until Lewis's death.

Lewis submitted the portrait to the Royal Academy annual exhibition in 1938. It was rejected by the Hanging Committee, and Augustus John's resultant resignation, in protest, led to a furore in the press. There was much heated correspondence over the 'rejected portrait', as it came to be known,

143

144

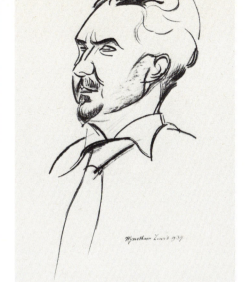

145

146

and Lewis found himself at the centre of a public controversy. Winston Churchill, principal speaker at the Academy's annual dinner, devoted a large proportion of his address to the subject, coming down in favour of the Academy. The picture was displayed briefly at the Lefevre Gallery, where it was viewed by many, before being sold to the Durban Art Gallery.

It is perhaps surprising that Lewis chose to enter a picture into the Royal Academy at all. He had repeatedly attacked the institution as being responsible for what he considered to be the amateurish and second-rate quality of much of British art. However, it is characteristic of Lewis's contradictory personality. Also, his occasional attempts to earn money and popularity in the established art world may have prompted his action. The 'rejected portrait' controversy probably took everyone by surprise, including Lewis. In a letter to the editor of *The Times* of 5 May 1938, Lewis argued defensively and provocatively: 'somebody had to stop the Academy from eternally protesting that all the good artists were outside because they never sent in!'[2]

On 21 April 1938, Eliot wrote to Lewis: 'so far as the sitter is able to judge, it seems to me a very good portrait, and one by which I am quite willing that posterity should know me, if it takes any interest in me at all.'[3]

[1] *B & B*, p.282
[2] Quoted in W.Lewis, *Wyndham Lewis the Artist: from Blast to Burlington House*, 1939, pp.379–80
[3] *Letters*, p.251

Durban Art Gallery, South Africa

148

Four Figure Composition

1938
Oil on canvas
$19\frac{1}{2} \times 15\frac{1}{2}$ (49·5 × 39·5)
Signed: *Wyndham Lewis 1938*
Coll: Sir Nicholas Waterhouse; Agnes Bedford; Mrs A.F.Tsciffeley
Michel (P81)

An example of the theme of players on a stage which occurs frequently in Lewis's work, for example, *The Audition* and *Abstract: Ballet Scene* (see cat.23, 135). A row of stage lights can be seen at top left and two of the figures stand in the beam of spotlights. Similar swirling and spiralling forms occur in the background of *Portrait of T.S.Eliot* (cat.147).

Private Collection

148

149

150

149

Josephine Plummer

1939
Oil on canvas
$29\frac{1}{2} \times 19\frac{1}{2}$ (75 × 49·5)
Unsigned
Michel (P97)

The sitter was working in the BBC Drama
Department when she was introduced to
Lewis by E.W.F.Tomlin, the writer and
critic, and another friend who thought that
Lewis would like to paint her long face and
sharply cut profile. The sittings took place
in Lewis's Notting Hill Gate studio. Lewis
told her that he was planning to save
enough money by the sale of this and other
portraits to go to America, which he did
later that year.

Mrs Josephine Whitehorn

151

150

Figure Falling from a Horse

1941
Pen and ink, watercolour
$11\frac{1}{2} \times 17\frac{5}{8}$ (29 × 45)
Signed: *W Lewis. 1941.*
Coll: Mrs Anne Wyndham Lewis
Michel (977)

A sinister, disturbing composition, done during Lewis's desolate years in Canada. It includes a stunted, recumbent figure, an image which occurs frequently in Lewis's work, for example, *Manhattan* (cat.106), and *Figures in the Air* (cat.105). The image of horse and rider also appears frequently in Lewis's imaginative drawings. The cover design for *The Enemy No.1* shows a threatening armoured figure on horseback (see also Michel 622, 631, 634, 970, 1103). These drawings have a personal significance for the artist and are reminiscent of Lewis's description in *The Wild Body* stories of his own form as: 'This forked, strange-scented, blond-skinned gut-bag, with its two bright rolling marbles with which it sees, bull's-eyes full of mockery and madness, is my stalking-horse. I hang somewhere in its midst operating it with detachment.'[1]

[1] W.Lewis, *The Wild Body*, 1927, p.5

C.J.Fox

151

Bathers

1942
Pencil and watercolour
10 × 15 (25·5 × 38)
Signed: *Wyndham Lewis 1942*
Michel (992)

One of a series of drawings of bathers from the years 1941–2 which was inspired by a collection of paintings by Etty in the house of a Toronto industrialist.[1]

[1] see Michel (P104, 986, 991, 993, 994)

Victoria and Albert Museum (Circ.421–1959)

152

Creation Myth
also called Landscape

1944
Black and coloured chalks
11 × $14\frac{1}{2}$ (28 × 37)
Signed: *Wyndham Lewis 1944*
Michel (1045)

A fantastic and whimsical sketch done during the Canadian period.

Private Collection

152

153

153

Negro Heaven

1946
Pen, black and coloured chalks
$19\frac{1}{2} \times 14$ (49·5 × 35·5)
Signed: *Wyndham Lewis 1946*
Michel (1081)

In a number of drawings of the late 1940s when Lewis's eyesight was rapidly fading, forms become smaller and heavily worked, and appear scattered at random over the page. The whole effect gives more the appearance of a doodle than a finished drawing. *Negro Heaven* was the only drawing produced in America during the war years to be included in the Redfern Gallery exhibition of 1949.

Glasgow Art Gallery and Museum

154

The Nativity

1949
Pen and ink, pencil, coloured chalks, watercolour
$11\frac{1}{4} \times 17\frac{1}{2}$ (28·5 × 44·5)
Signed (in pencil, erased): *Wyndham Lewis 1941*
Signed (in ink): *Wyndham Lewis 1949*
Michel (1099)

The drawing was probably begun in 1941 at the same time as a similar work, *Adoration* (Michel 963) and completed in 1949. The figures appear to be acting on a stage with stage props filling the background. The rather uneven quality of the work testifies to Lewis's approaching blindness.

With the Mayor Gallery, London

155

French Soldiers Carrying Babies and Visiting Graves

1951
Pen and coloured inks, watercolour, gouache
$12\frac{1}{2} \times 15$ (32 × 38)
Signed: *WL 1951.*
Michel (1127)

Lewis signed and dated the work when it was acquired by the present owner, and it may have been executed as far back as the early 1940s. It was a work that he particularly liked.

Private Collection

154

155

156–9 are not by Lewis.

156 Horace Brodzky (1885–1969)

Viewing Kermesse

1917
Drypoint
$4\frac{5}{8} \times 3\frac{3}{4}$ (11 × 9·5)
Signed: *HB 1917* and in pencil: *Horace Brodzky*
Inscr: THE VORTICIST EXHIBITION / AT THE
PENGUIN GALLERY / NEW YORK JAN. 1917

The only record of Lewis's lost painting
Kermesse, first exhibited at the Allied
Artists' Association summer salon in 1912
with the title *Creation* (see cat.14).[1]

[1] see Cork, p.37f.

Victoria and Albert Museum

156

157 Augustus John (1878–1961)

Portrait of Wyndham Lewis

c.1903
Etching and drypoint
$6\frac{15}{16} \times 5\frac{7}{16}$ (17·7 × 13·9)
Signed: *John 1893* [incorrectly dated]

Augustus John and Lewis were life-long
friends. They first met early on in Lewis's
career, probably while Lewis was still a
student at the Slade (see cat.1). From
1903–8, they saw much of each other. This
early portrait is one of two etchings after the
charcoal drawing of Lewis by John, signed
and dated 1903 (formerly belonging to Mrs
Anne Wyndham Lewis, repr. *Letters*, p.9).

Private Collection

157

158

158 Augustus John (1878–1961)

Portrait of Wyndham Lewis

c.1905
Oil on canvas
$31\frac{1}{2} \times 24 \ (80 \times 61)$
Signed: *John*

Lewis, during his student years in Paris, assumed the rôle of a bohemian artist and poet, and dressed in a suitably theatrical manner. In his autobiography, *Chiaroscuro*, John wrote: 'In the cosmopolitan world of Montparnasse, P.Wyndham Lewis played the part of an incarnate loki, bearing the news and sowing discord with it. He conceived the world as an arena, where various insurrectionary forces struggled to outwit each other in the game of artistic power politics. Impatient of quietude, star-gazing or wool-gathering, our new Machiavelli sought to ginger up his friends, or patients as they might be called, by a whisper here, a dark suggestion there.'[1]

[1] Augustus John, *Chiaroscuro*, 1952, p.73

Private Collection

159 Michael Ayrton (1921–1975)

Portrait Study of Wyndham Lewis

1955
Pencil on paper
$10 \times 14 \ (25 \cdot 4 \times 35 \cdot 5)$
Unsigned

A study for the oil portrait of the blind Lewis painted in 1955 (Private Collection). Ayrton first met Lewis in 1946. Their mutual admiration for each other's work led to a professional collaboration. Ayrton wrote the catalogue foreword to Lewis's 1949 exhibition at the Redfern Gallery and in 1953, Ayrton was commissioned to design the dust-jacket for Lewis's novel *Self-Condemned* and later illustrated the second and third volumes of Lewis's *The Human Age*. Ayrton described Lewis as 'clothed in black ... hunched in a blue-black chair squared off, partner to his ashtray and on the summit of Mr Lewis's black and formal figure was Mr Lewis's head, wedge-shaped, blade-nosed, with a forehead like a sledgehammer beneath which the girders of his spectacle-frames seemed to provide a dangerous cakewalk [*sic*] for ideas to cross.' Lewis, when blind, wore a green plastic peak which 'added a curious dimension to his face. The forehead which hitherto had been, it seemed to me, designed for striking ringing blows, was now bisected but armed with a green obsidian cutting edge from beneath which the nose reared like a secret weapon; an armed head indeed.'
(M.Ayrton, *Golden Sections*, London, 1957, pp.148, 151.)

Mrs Elisabeth Ayrton

159

Lenders

Private Collections
Penelope Allen   131
Mrs Elisabeth Ayrton   159
Ivor Braka   6
The Fine Art Society Ltd   123
C.J.Fox   8, 150
David W.Hughes   122
The Maclean Gallery   82
The Mayor Gallery   154
Chris and Oriole Mullen   136
New College, Oxford, Junior Common Room   121
Anthony d'Offay   40, 42, 43, 86, 132
Graham Peacock   128
Pembroke College, Oxford, Junior Common Room   74
Private Collection   4, 5, 14, 17, 19, 27, 28, 31, 32, 34, 37, 41, 56, 83, 85, 94, 97, 98, 99, 100, 101, 102, 103, 109, 119, 125, 137, 138, 148, 152, 155, 157, 158
Slade School of Fine Art, University College, London   1
Julian Symons   146
The Vint Trust   9, 62, 77, 87, 95, 105, 106, 108, 124, 126, 142, 144
Dame Rebecca West   111
Mrs Josephine Whitehorn   149
W.D. & H.O.Wills   134

Public Collections
Aberdeen Art Gallery and Museums   117
Bedford, The Trustees of the Cecil Higgins Art Gallery   10, 89, 127
Bradford Art Galleries and Museums   135
City of Bristol Museum and Art Gallery   139
Cambridge, The Syndics of the Fitzwilliam Museum   110
Cardiff, The National Museum of Wales   61
Carlisle Museum and Art Gallery   140
Durban Art Gallery, South Africa   147
Edinburgh, Scottish National Gallery of Modern Art   81, 92
Glasgow Art Gallery and Museum   133, 153
Harrogate Borough Council Art Gallery   84
Kettering, The Alfred East Art Gallery   114
Kingston-upon-Hull, Ferens Art Gallery   80
Leeds City Art Galleries   79
London, The Arts Council of Great Britain   20, 53, 116
London, The Courtauld Institute of Art   29
London, The National Portrait Gallery   88, 96, 112
London, The Trustees of the Imperial War Museum   48, 49

Photograph credits

The Right Worshipful The Lord Mayor
Councillor Mrs Winifred Smith

Chairman
Councillor R. W. Ford

Deputy Chairman
Councillor Mrs S. V. Shaw

Councillor D. Barker
Councillor Mrs M. I. Crawford
Councillor N. I. Finley
Councillor M. Harrison
Councillor K. McKeon, JP
Councillor C. McLaren
Councillor Miss M. Pierce
Councillor H. B. Smith
Councillor R. E. Talbot
Councillor M. J. Taylor
Councillor A. C. Thomas
Councillor Miss M. A. Vince, JP
Professor C. R. Dodwell, MA, PhD
Mr H. M. Fairhurst, MA, FRIBA
Mr G. N. C. Flint, MA, LLB
Mr G. North, MA
Dr F. W. Ratcliffe, MA, PhD, JP
Professor K. R. Richards, MA
Mr C. G. H. Simon, MA, JP

Director of Cultural Services
L. G. Lovell, FLA

Director of Art Galleries
T. P. P. Clifford, BA, AMA